The Romance
Readers' Advisory

ALA READERS' ADVISORY SERIES

The Short Story Readers' Advisory:
A Guide to the Best

The Romance Readers' Advisory

The Librarian's Guide to Love in the Stacks

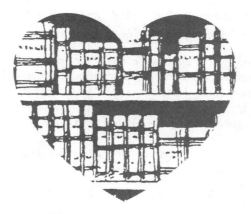

Ann Bouricius

AMERICAN LIBRARY ASSOCIATION
Chicago and London
2000

Cover design: Lucy Lesiak Design

Text design: Dianne M. Rooney

Composition by the dotted i using Berkeley and Snell Roundhand using QuarkXPress 4.04 on a Macintosh platform

Printed on 50-pound white offset, a pH-neutral stock, and bound in 10-point coated cover stock by McNaughton & Gunn

The paper used in this publication meets the minimum requirements of American National Standard for Information Sciences—Permanence of Paper for Printed Library Materials, ANSI Z39.48-1992. ♾

Library of Congress Cataloging-in-Publication Data
Bouricius, Ann
    The romance readers' advisory : the librarian's guide to love in the stacks / Ann Bouricius.
        p.   cm.
    ISBN 0-8389-0779-2
    1. Love stories, American—Bibliography—Methodology.   2. Love stories, English—Bibliography—Methodology.   3. Libraries—Special collections—Love stories.   4. Love stories—Stories, plots, etc.
    5. Love stories—Appreciation.   6. Reading interests.   I. Title.
    Z1231.L68 B68 2000
    [PS374.L6]
    016.813'085—dc21   99-057295

Printed in the United States of America

04   03   02   01   00   5   4   3   2   1

Contents

6

7

Appendixes

Index

Acknowledgments

Thank you to the many people who talked to me, answered my questions, and allowed me to quote them: Carol Vantresca; Ann Taylor; John Charles; Leslie Haas; Paula Eykelhoff; Zilla Soriano; the lovely people at the Romance Writers of America offices; Pam Baker, who is always present at the conception of my books; Stephanie Mittman; Mary Jo Putney; Laurie Grant; Sue Krinard; Lorraine Heath; Vince Brach; Linda Markowiak; Victoria Alexander; Alice Duncan; Madeline Baker; Susan Grant; Jean Brashear; Peggy Moreland; Susan Wiggs; Patricia Potter; Karen Harper; Deborah Simmons; Paula Detmer Riggs; and Jennifer Greene.

Thank you to my family, who put up with too many nights of fast food.

Thank you to the many librarians all over the country who are romance readers and proud.

And most of all, thank you to Sherry for bullying me into reading my first romance.

Introduction

In which I tell the story of my own path of enlightenment from paper-trained snob to closet convert to blazing zealot and romance author.

I graduated from the University of Illinois Graduate School of Library and Information Science in June of 1984 and moved to Columbus, Ohio, to begin my career as a children's services librarian. I was very proud of my title. Librarian. That word held magic for me. It meant books, and in my life, books were good.

Libraries have been a given in my life since I was old enough to scribble my name on my own library card. When I was young, going to the library each week was as much a part of my life as breathing. And when I graduated from library school and held that piece of paper in my hot little hand, I had arrived. I was going to inspire kids by introducing them to great books, as librarians had inspired me. This was my mission. I took myself very seriously and was probably fairly pompous at times.

One day, a fellow librarian suggested I read a book by Patricia Veryan. I'm sure I turned my nose up at the thought of reading "one of those bodice busters." After all, I was a paper-trained librarian. I read *real* books. I had standards. But my fellow librarian was persistent. "Just read the first couple of chapters," she said. "Then, if you don't like it, don't finish it."

I stood firm, secure in my belief that I was above such pabulum. She also stood firm and shoved Veryan's books at me for months. Finally, one day, I knew I'd see her at a meeting the next afternoon, and I knew she'd start her bullying again. So I decided I'd read the first chapter of the blasted book, just to get her to shut up about it.

That night I put my two boys to bed, sat down with the wretched book, and opened to the first page. I finished the book, *The Lord and the Gypsy,* at about three in the morning. Far from being the mindless pap I'd thought romances were, I found Veryan's book to be full of adventure and buckling swash, with strong women and dashing men and villains that got their come-uppance. I loved it. It was terrific. I wanted more. The next day, I checked out everything that my branch owned by Veryan, and placed reserves for the rest. Of course I did this surreptitiously, not wanting the rest of the library staff to know I was reading "those books." When I finished *Sanguinet's Crown,* the last in Veryan's Regency series, I was totally bereft. I felt as if I'd lost my best friends.

So I began reading Regencies by other authors and then moved on to Regency historicals and medievals. I still didn't know what all the differences and sub-genres were, and I didn't care. I only knew that I liked what I was reading, even though I read them at home so no one would know.

I was a closet romance reader for about a year when one day, an elderly woman was at the circulation desk checking out a stack of romances. On top of her pile was a Candlelight Ecstasy Supreme by Emily Elliott called *Just His Touch.* Without thinking, I said, "Oh, that one is *so* good. I cried buckets over it last night!"

The woman looked at me and her eyes grew round and wide. "You read these books, too?" she asked incredulously. She said "these books" as if she was embarrassed for reading romances and at the same time apologetic for liking them—and astounded that a librarian would read them also.

I do not know who that woman was, and I never saw her again, but she changed my life. That moment was, for me, an epiphany. Why should this woman, or anyone else, have to feel apologetic for liking romances? Why should she be embarrassed to read them? Evidently, *I* was embarrassed to read romances be-cause I still did it secretly. Was I one of the people who had made this lady feel apologetic? I took a good look at myself. Why did I care what other people thought of what I read? I was not, I realized, being honest. I was worse than a snob. I was two-faced. Pretending to disparage romances during the day, while secretly devouring them at night. Well, no more! From that moment I was out of the romance-reading closet forever. Proudly I read romances in public, brandishing them like a sword, flaunting them like a flag. I was brazen. I was brave. I was a librarian. I read romances. And I was proud.

From reading romances, it was a series of many small steps that led me to try writing one, just to see if I could do it. I joined Romance Writers of America—my birthday present to myself one year, learned to use a computer, and sat down to begin a book.

Writing a romance is not the quick little toss-off thing people often think it is. You really can't whip one out in a weekend, no matter what anyone says. It took me two years to write my first book, to learn the process of writing a romance. I finished that one, and, having fallen under the spell of writing, started the next one. Writing was, for me, as addicting as chocolate. I sold the third book I wrote, along with a proposal for another. Since then, I've sold several more.

I am thrilled to write this particular book. It is written for all the public librarians in the country who read romances on the sly, for all those who read romances openly, for all those who have ever turned their nose up at a romance, and for all those who are faced with the task of building or maintaining a romance collection and are totally lost. Also it's for those who would like to create a romance collection in their libraries and want some ammunition to take to their directors.

1

A Tour of the Romance Genre

No More Heaving Bosoms

The Popularity of Romances

Six every second, 383 every minute, 23,006 every hour, 552,156 every day, 3,875,712 every week, 16,794,750 every month, 201,537,000 for the year. That's how romance books were selling in the United States in 1997. Think of it. More than two hundred million romances were sold in 1997. These figures only include sales of new books. There are no figures from used bookstores, which do a booming business in secondhand romance paperbacks.

Statistical information on the romance genre was published in the June 1999 issue of *Romance Writers' Report,* the publication of Romance Writers of America. Romances accounted for "37.5% of all Adult Popular Fiction books sold, which includes hardcover, trade paperbacks and mass-market (also called rack-size) paperbacks." Just for perspective, "other categories were: Mystery, Detective, Espionage and Suspense, 24.9%, General, 16%, Science Fiction and Fantasy, 8.1%. The remainder, 13.3% included Religious, Occult, Male Adventure, Historical, Western, Adult and Movie Tie-ins" (p. 21). When we take out the hardbacks and trade paperbacks and only look at mass-market adult popular fiction paperbacks, romance accounts for 53 percent of the books sold.

2

A TOUR OF THE ROMANCE GENRE

In 1998, 1,963 new and reissued romance titles were published. Contrary to popular belief, romances are not all alike. It is important for conscientious librarians to understand this genre so we can make intelligent purchasing decisions. We librarians do try to maintain a diverse general fiction collection. We try to have a broad selection of books for our readers. We owe it to our romance readers to have a romance collection that is just as broad and diverse as our collection of general fiction.

It is my intent to describe the romance genre as it is today and how we as librarians can best incorporate romances into our collections. I have taken the liberty of referring to romance readers as "she" in this book. I know there are men who read romances. However, since the vast majority of readers are women, and since the "she or he" construction is clumsy, please indulge me.

I am also not going to spend much time discussing electronic publishing. Even though many electronic publishers are springing up on the Web, I believe that currently romances published electronically are not a practical purchase for libraries building a romance collection. This has more to do with the current level of technology than the books themselves. Currently, e-books can be purchased either on disk or by download and can be read on a computer or on a handheld reader. However, there is no universal formatting. Most readers can only read text in one of several specific formats. Also, as yet there is no test of time for e-publishers. Anyone with the technical know-how can create a Web page, call themselves a publisher, and accept manuscripts. Then there is the issue of public downloading rights. Eventually, these things will work themselves out. The legitimate e-publishers will consistently produce quality books; the others will not. Eventually formatting issues will resolve themselves until there is a universal format. How many of us remember the days of Beta v. VHS videotapes? So until the technology and legalities have progressed to a level where such purchases are practical for public libraries, we can read about e-books on the Web.

So, on to romance. What are these books that are selling so well?

What Are Romances? They're Not about Sex

They're not about sex. Let me repeat that. Romances are not about sex. Often when we hear the term "romance" referring to a genre book, we instantly think of sex—and it's usually accompanied by a knowingly sly *wink, wink.* In fact, many of the pejorative slang terms referring to romances have to do with sex. "Thrust and lust," "smut books," "bodice rippers" (have you ever tried to rip a bodice?). We are smug in our certitude that these fluffy little books are nothing more than a series of quick tumbles ending with a "wham-bam-thank-you-ma'am." We are so certain of our opinions that few of us have actually ever read a romance to find out if we're right. Well, we're wrong. Romances are women's fantasies, and most women I know don't have fantasies about nameless, faceless sex.

Well, if they're not about sex, then what are they about? Romances are about a developing monogamous relationship between a man and a woman. Romances are about what it takes to make a relationship work. Romances are about women making choices in their lives. Romances are about overcoming serious obstacles and coming out on the other side stronger for the struggle. Romances are about women winning.

For a book to qualify as a romance in the purest genre sense, the focus of the book must be the developing relationship between the heroine and hero. I often say that the relationship itself is the main character of a romance. Women's fiction, on the other hand, focuses on a particular woman or women. She may have one or more romantic relationships during the course of the book, but the focus is on her, not her relationships. This is why most of Danielle Steel's books are women's fiction, not romance. In women's fiction, the woman does not have to necessarily "get her man," as in a romance. In women's fiction, she may realize that the man she thought was Mr. Wonderful is really Mr. Scuzzy. Or she may find that what she really wants to do is spend the rest of her life working with orphaned orangutans in the jungles of Borneo. In women's fiction, these are both perfectly fine ways to end a book because women's fiction is about the *woman* rather than the *relationship*. Romances are about the relationship. While women's fiction stories may be romantic, they are not romances. They are not supposed to be.

Romance has other requirements that set it apart from women's fiction. In a romance, the relationship is monogamous; neither the hero nor heroine can die; and there must be an HEA, a happily-ever-after, ending. Most importantly of all, both hero and heroine are heroic. They must be basically good people. They must be people readers can care about and cheer on.

We often criticize romances for not being about reality. And deep down we also often wonder if the women who read romances don't know reality from fantasy. Historical romance writer Madeline Baker was called for jury duty. During the jury selection process one of the attorneys asked her what she did for a living. She told him she wrote romances. Then, in all seriousness, the attorney asked her, "Ms. Baker, do you know the difference between reality and fantasy?"

The answer is a resounding yes. Women who write romances and women who read them do know the difference between reality and fantasy. When I want hard cold reality I watch the evening news or I read the newspaper. When I want to relax and escape into a life-affirming story where I know there will be a happy ending, I read a romance. Romance author Paula Detmer Riggs has said that romances give us a glimpse of what the world would be like if we were all nice, honorable people. The evening news tends to celebrate the tragedies in the world. Romances celebrate the life. I choose life.

So, in a romance, who is this love relationship with? Sometimes the heroine learns that the true hero is the proverbial guy next door, as in Stephanie Mittman's *A Kiss to Dream On*. Sometimes she finds an old flame she thought she'd never see again, as in Jennifer Crusie's *Tell Me Lies*. She might find herself running for her life accompanied by a man she doesn't know whether she can trust, as in Eileen Wilks' *Proposition: Marriage*. However she finds him, find him she does. Then she goes through the pain of almost losing him again. This is usually when she learns what he means to her. There is a last-minute reprieve followed by a happily-ever-after ending. More about heroes and HEA endings later.

Romances are also about people growing and changing. Facing seemingly insurmountable challenges and finding the strength and courage to conquer them. A crucible, as it were. We want to put base metal into a fiery crucible and have it come out as pure gold. So it is with our characters. They go through whatever their fire is and they come out on the other side better people. When she goes through her fire and finds her happily-ever-after ending, the woman wins. Romances are about women winning. As Deborah Smith once said, "In romances, the woman always ends up on top." This inner growth of character is as much a part of the HEA ending as the romantic commitment. In fact, without this growth, in whatever form it comes, there cannot be an HEA ending.

So what's all the fuss about sex? Sex happens. Often in a romance, as in many real-life relationships, a couple decides to physically commit themselves to each other. Yes, there are still some captor/captive romances where the physical relationship may come before an emotional commitment, though these storylines are not as common as they once were. But because the reader knows this is a romance, she knows the man and woman will fall in love. A consummated relationship, by the way, is not a required element of a romance novel. Some lines require the couple to wait until after they are married to consummate their relationship. But remember monogamy. Once the heroine meets the hero and their romance begins, there is usually no sexual interaction with anyone else for either of them. There are, of course, exceptions, but this is a general rule of the romance. The reader also knows that when the two characters commit themselves to each other, they will remain together forever. Why do we know this? Because they have proved themselves to be worthy.

The level of sensuality—the degree to which the author describes the desire and, if appropriate, consummation—varies from line to line, from author to author, from story to story. Romances are usually described as being sweet, mildly sensual, sensual, highly sensual, steamy, or explicit.

Several years ago there was a book that was on all the best-seller lists, and the reserve list was a mile long. It was not a romance, but I decided I should read it for my own professional growth and for the good of my soul. I forget the title, but the cover was yellow and it was toward the end of the *S*s in the middle of the row. The author was a man who had written several books. His books were usually well reviewed. The main character was a wealthy tycoon who was into rough, recreational sex and used women as objects for his personal pleasure and sex as a means of controlling them. He referred to the women he had sex with as "the blonde," or "the one with the short brown hair." Now, the writing style was decent. The sex was rough and graphic and devoid of any emotional content. The plot was as deep as it had to be, but no deeper. Yet this book was, and still is, regarded as quality fiction.

On the other hand, a romance that is about a committed relationship between two people who struggle to become stronger in order to develop that relationship is seen as fluff. Is seen as damaging. Is seen as trash. What's wrong with this picture?

What is wrong with this picture is that we as a society have preconceived notions of what a romance novel is and is not. We are basing our opinions on incorrect and flawed information.

They're Not All Alike; or, Formula Is Not a Four-Letter Word

Formula! We use it as a swear word and point and snigger. Before my own enlightenment, I used to make jokes that in every romance the hero and heroine met on page 10, had a passionate kiss on page 17, and by page 34 they were—well, you know, *wink, wink*. I was wrong. I have current tip sheets from all major romance publishers, and in none of them do the editors say that by page 34 the hero and heroine must be engaged in—well, you know, *wink, wink.*

So what is this all about? What's this formula that's supposed to exist? Is there one? Yes, there is. There is a formula to a romance.

There is also a formula to a symphony, a fugue, a mystery, a sonnet, a haiku, a limerick. There is even a formula to a knock-knock joke. We expect a limerick to be heavily metered and have a specific rhythm. A knock-knock joke always begins, "Knock, knock. Who's there?" Haiku have a specific number of beats to each line, as do sonnets. These are perfectly acceptable in polite society. I don't think I've ever heard anyone bash Elizabeth Barrett Browning because her *Sonnets from the Portuguese* are formulaic.

So let's look at this F-word thing. A formula is simply a pattern, a structure. Within the boundaries of this pattern, this structure, an author tells her story. Purely as an example, let us think of formula as the basic requirements for a house. For a house we need a door, a roof, probably some windows and walls, and, at least in my opinion, indoor plumbing. This is our formula. Now, we take our formula and build a house. I can guarantee that if you build a house and I build a house, even though we are using exactly that same formula, they will look nothing alike.

In the romance genre the structure is fairly simple. Some writers begin their ideas for a story with a man. My stories begin with a woman or with a dog. So, beginning with a woman, here we go with the official romance formula:

THE OFFICIAL ROMANCE FORMULA

Woman meets man.

Woman realizes she likes man and man likes her.

Woman loses man.

Woman gets man.

They live happily ever after.

There are three things to note in this highly simplified structure. First, there's nothing about what's supposed to happen on page 17 or on any other page. Second, everything is about the relationship between the woman and the man. Third, there is a happily-ever-after ending. Incidentally, this year I'm reading men's action novels. (It's on my personal action plan, which you will read about later.) The books I've read so far have followed this same formula except that instead of a heroine and hero, men's action novels are stories between a good guy and a bad guy and when they come together instead of exchanging kisses they exchange gunshots. There comes a moment in the end where the bad guy appears to have gotten away. Then, at the very last minute, the good guy gets the bad guy. But instead of a great passionate love scene, there's a scene full of explosions and things blowing up. It's the same formula. This is also the same formula used in many movies that are romantic comedies, such as *While You Were Sleeping.*

Why is this formula thing important to librarians? Readers' advisory. A reader who is looking for a narrative poem does not want a book of limericks. A reader who is looking for limericks will not be impressed if we give her a book of haiku. Likewise, a reader who is looking for a romance will not be happy if we give her women's fiction and call it romance. First of all, we are not giving her what she wants. Secondly, we show our own ignorance and insult her reading taste by implying that the difference between women's fiction and romance is not important. We have a professional responsibility to our library users to know what makes a romance a romance. And that is why formula is important.

As an author of popular fiction, this structure or formula is important because it gives me a ready-made shape to my story. I also think that is why so many romance writers are able to write new books fairly quickly. We don't have to invent a new path every time we start a new book. I know that Liz and Alex are going to end up together and are going to almost lose each other along the way. The how-they-get-there is what is important; the where-they-are-going is understood.

Formula is important to a reader because of something called reader expectation. Readers expect certain things from certain forms of literature. They have a right to expect that a limerick will be a limerick and not turn into something else in the last line. We are familiar with the form of a limerick, and as we hear the last line, it resolves correctly. There is a kind of comfort in this. We knew what to expect, so we anticipated it, we got it, and all is right with the world.

In the same way, as a romance reader, formula is important because I know there will be a crucible and then an HEA ending. When I'm reading a romance, I want to identify strongly with the characters, care about them, cry with them, and rejoice with them. I don't want to pick up a book and invest lots of time and emotion in the characters only to come to the ending and find they're wrong for each other. Or find one of them is killed. When Philip Pullman killed off one of my favorite characters in the end of *The Shadow in the North* (which is not a romance but still a terrific read until you get to the ending), I was so furious I stomped up and down my front porch for ten minutes saying all manner of evil things against Pullman. It was eight years before I read another book by him. I didn't trust him. He had made me care about someone and then killed him.

Romance writers want their readers to care about the characters. We use certain techniques, such as point of view, to foster this caring. Point of view, when done correctly, allows readers to get inside the head of the characters, to see the world through their eyes. This enables readers to strongly identify with the characters. In this way, the reader goes with the character into the crucible, feels that character's pain. Readers are willing to do this because they know that after the darkness there will be sunshine. There will be a light at the end of the tunnel. This faith in the light is a trust between writer and reader, and romance writers do not take it casually. This is why formula is important.

Romances Have Heroines and Heroes

Heroines of today's romance novels are women who survive, who grow and change, who go through the fire and come out on the other end stronger for the struggle. While in the early days of genre romance heroines were often virginal and passive, today's heroines are not. Romance heroines written today are pilots, farmers, entrepreneurs, journalists, single mothers, or doctors. I've written about a veterinarian, a rubber stamp artist, an attorney, a car mechanic, and a librarian. Currently, I'm writing about a kindergarten teacher. Granted, characters in historical novels have fewer career choices due to the constraints of history. However, even historical heroines are women in their own right, rather than mere pawns.

Today's heroines are women who have a life. When life shoves them around, they learn when and how it is appropriate to shove back. When life gives them lemons they might make lemonade; then again, they might return them to the grocery store for a refund. When they are in trouble, rather than waiting for a man to rescue them, they rescue themselves. Sometimes, along the way, they even rescue the man. These women are not victims. They are women we, the readers, admire. They are the kind of women we want for our friends. They are the kind of women we want to be.

Nan Springfield, in Stephanie Mittman's *Head over Heels,* is the widow of a minister who died suddenly after being accused of embezzling church funds. Along with facing the accusations of her husband's embezzlement and his death, she is about to lose her house and she finds out that one of her three foster children is autistic and the man she has begun to care for may not be who she thinks he is. This is the beginning of a series of crises in her life. But instead of taking on an "oh, woe is me," attitude, she does what she can to pull her life together. When she becomes so tired of fighting that she allows a trusted relative to make decisions for her and learns that person is not to be trusted after all, Nan finds the inner strength to stand up proudly for her moral scruples. Because of her struggles, she has learned that she is stronger than she ever knew she was.

Francine Rivers' 1994 novel, *Redeeming Love,* is another example of a strong woman's growth. Angel, the heroine, is a soiled dove, a lady of the night, a prostitute. The hero is a farmer, a truly good man who believes in a God of forgiveness and redemption. He falls in love with her, but her self-esteem has been trampled for so long that she is unable to accept his love. It is only when she pulls herself out of her working life and finds a sense of dignity and of her own self-worth that she is able to come to him as an equal and accept his love. Note that Rivers recently revised her novel for the Inspirational market, and it was reissued by Multnomah.

So-called experts often state that romance novels are responsible for keeping women subservient and in abusive relationships. I am truly confused by this. No self-respecting romance heroine would stay in an abusive relationship. That is simply not the stuff of romance. She may begin the book in such a situation, but, believe me, before the book is finished she'll be out of it and with a whole new sense of her own self. The only conclusion I can draw from this faulty claim is that these so-called experts have not read *Head over Heels,* or *Redeeming Love,* or any other current romance recently.

Obviously, since heroines are strong women, their heroes must be their equals. Today's heroes can be single dads who know how to change diapers and do it. They can be helicopter pilots, U.S. Marshals, talk-show radio hosts, knights, or warriors. Sometimes they're even virgins. I've written about an elementary school principal, a designer of computer games, a mailman, a school-bus driver, and a man who renovates old houses. The hero of my current novel-in-progress trains service dogs. In historicals, heroes may be dukes or sea captains. They may be officers on leave from the Napoleonic wars or young knights setting off for the Crusades. They may be farmers or ranchers settling the West. Whatever their occupation or station in life, heroes are heroic. They rescue kittens from trees and help little old ladies cross the street. Sometimes a hero hides these deeds from all the other characters in the book; after all, he doesn't want to appear to be a softie. But the reader has seen him save the kitten, and she knows he's heroic and worthy of the heroine.

Readers and also writers sometimes try to categorize heroes into types. A reader will say that she likes "alpha" heroes, or she likes "beta" heroes. It would be impossible and impractical for librarians to know every single hero type and know what books they appear in. Quite often readers even disagree about what type a particular hero is. It is an inexact science. Most simply put, when someone says "alpha" hero, think Mel Gibson in *Braveheart.* When someone says "beta" hero, think Jimmy Stewart in *It's a Wonderful Life.* William Wallace and George Bailey are totally different types; yet in his own way, each is splendid and heroic.

Harlequin Is Not a Generic Term

Before I became converted to romances, I used the word "Harlequin" as a generic term, one of those words like Kleenex and Jello and Kitty Litter that refers to all of its kind rather than to a specific name brand. After all, I didn't know any better. I was ignorant even of my own ignorance.

Each of the two major publishers of category romance, Harlequin and Silhouette, actually publish several lines, or categories, of romances that are very different from each other. Each of these category lines comes out with a certain number of books each month. The books are numbered sequentially within the line and each line has a distinctive look. These are referred to as category books, or series romances. These are short books, ranging from 40,000 to 75,000 words, depending on the line.

In the romance world, the term "series book" most often refers to a book from one of the Silhouette or Harlequin lines. However, there are also limited continuing series, those we usually think of as series, within category lines. For instance, Rachel Lee writes a continuing series for Silhouette called Conard County. These books are all set in a small Wyoming town and have continuing characters. Laurie Grant writes a series for Harlequin Historicals in which each book is about a different member of the Devlin family. Some lines also publish multiauthor series, such as Harlequin Historicals' *Knights of the Black Rose,* a sequence of books about a group of friends home from the Crusades.

Category lines evolve and change, rise and fall, based on the publishers' perception of reader demand or lack of it. Silhouette's Shadows line, a series of paranormal stories, folded due to the publisher's perceived lack of reader response. Bantam's Loveswept series recently folded after fifteen years. On the other side, Kensington has just developed a new line of contemporary category romance.

When it comes to category romance, each book within a certain line has a similar feel, a similar flavor. To use the house analogy again, a Harlequin Temptation would probably be a condo, while a Harlequin Superromance would probably be a two-story ranch with a huge tree in the front yard. Category lines have been described as a community. The reader recognizes this and becomes part of that community. This is very important in terms of reader expectation. Some readers read almost exclusively in one line. Some readers read across lines. However they read them, serious series readers know what to expect from their books. There is a certain kind of comfort in this. For instance, when I'm horribly stressed or brain dead after a busy Saturday afternoon on the information desk during science fair season, I know that during my break I can pick up a Silhouette Romance and find a gentle and sweet read. I know that this book will help me keep my head when all about me are losing theirs.

One caveat. Even though there is a certain feel to each category line, these books are not cookie-cutter. All Cape Cods don't look alike, either. The basic house plan can be similar, but the builder uses landscape, location, and decoration to create a unique house. In the same way, each author uses this "feel" as a framework within which to write a unique story.

I believe libraries should have both the sweet category books and the hotter lines, as well as those in between. After all, our patrons need and deserve a choice. Category books can easily be placed on standing order.

Category Lines in Romance

Here is a brief summary of the general tone of each of the category lines as they are today.

Harlequin Romance   Harlequin Romance is characterized by warm, tender emotions, and the stories proceed at a gentle pace. The couple does not make love before they are emotionally committed, and even then the descriptions of lovemaking are not explicit.

Harlequin Presents   These books are glitzy and glamorous and can have an international flair. They have exceptionally masculine heroes who are gorgeous, powerful, sexy, and rich. They are provocative and show the excitement and drama of a passionate love affair. They may include explicit lovemaking.

Harlequin Temptation   This is Harlequin's most sensually explicit series. Some of the most explicit Temptations have a flash and the word *Blaze* in a circle on the cover and the spine. These are highly charged romances where almost anything goes. They may be humorous or topical or glitzy. They are always fast-paced with a very high level of sexual tension.

Harlequin Superromance   These are highly character-driven stories with depth and emotional intensity. Because a Super is longer, there is more time to explore the characters and develop subplots. Supers have a wide range of themes and a strong sense of place.

Harlequin American   These books are celebrations of love, life, and the American family. The adventurous hero and headstrong heroine are evenly matched people who meet the challenge of living in the current day. The stories are very upbeat.

Harlequin Intrigue   These are taut stories where suspense and romance are entwined. Both the hero and the heroine have a stake in the mystery. These are intensely sensual edge-of-your-seat stories. They are not issue-based.

Harlequin Duets   These are short romantic comedies with a high degree of sexual tension; however, love scenes are not a requirement of the line. Two books are bound into one volume.

Harlequin Historicals   In these stories, the romance overshadows the history. The level of sensuality varies from author to author. The stories take place before 1900. Though the most common settings are medieval, American West, and Regency periods, stories in other times and locales are published.

Silhouette Romance   These are sweet stories that emphasize emotions rather than sexuality. Although there is sexual tension, this is one of the lines where the couple does not make love until they are married. The stories are warm and dynamic and portray strong traditional family values. Silhouette Romance and Harlequin Romance are often referred to as *traditional romances*.

Silhouette Desire   These are short modern stories for readers who are comfortable with a high level of sensuality in their reading. They can be issue-based.

Silhouette Special Editions   These are longer romances with more character development and subplots. They are sophisticated, yet can have a more relaxed pace. The level of sensuality ranges from subtle to sizzling.

Silhouette Intimate Moments   These romances have a suspense element. Often the heroine or hero is in danger—and there is a clock ticking down to disaster. IMs are larger than life.

	HARLEQUIN LINE	SILHOUETTE LINE
Short and Sweet	Romance	Romance
Short and Spicy	Presents	Desire
Suspense	Intrigue	Intimate Moments
Highly Character-Driven	Superromance	Special Edition
Extremely Explicit	Temptation	
All-American	American	
Romantic Comedy	Duets	

Harlequin also has two lines, Bianca and Deseo, which are Spanish translations of their category romances. Bianca seems to be translations of sweeter romances, while Deseo appears to be translations of spicier romances.

Kensington is coming out with three new category lines. In mid-1999, they launched a new line of contemporary series romances called Bouquet. Kensington's Web site says these stories are "sensual romances with a vivid emotional tone, centered on strong characters, a dramatic conflict, and rich with sexual tension." They will also soon begin their Ballad line, which, according to their submission guidelines, "will consist entirely of two to six book series. There will be no stand-alone titles. These new miniseries may be written by one author, or several authors working together on a common concept."

Also new to Kensington is Encanto. According to their submission guidelines, these are short contemporary romances "with Hispanic characters and authentically reflecting U.S. Hispanic culture." Encanto characters do not make love until they are married. The interesting feature of Encanto romances is that they are "published in Spanish and English, with the texts in both languages in one mass-market volume." Four Encanto romances will be published every other month. Finally, Kensington recently launched Precious Gems, which are short contemporary romances available exclusively through Wal-Mart. A new historical line of Precious Gems will be out soon. It also will only be available through Wal-Mart.

Recently, Kensington sold their Arabesque line to Black Entertainment Television (BET). Arabesque publishes four romances each month. Arabesques "feature heroes and heroines of non-Caucasian heritage. We have published romances with predominately African-American characters up to this point." Other romances with non-Caucasian characters are published by Ballantine under their One World imprint.

Along with all the category romances, there are several other types of romances, each with individual style and flavor: Regencies, Regency historical, inspirational, romantic suspense, and paranormal romances. We'll begin with my first love, Regencies and Regency historical romances.

Regency v. Regency Historical Romance: What's in a Name?

I asked author Mary Jo Putney this question. Putney has written both Regencies and Regency historicals, so she seemed to be the perfect person to ask. She replied in an e-mail, "Technically the term Regency refers to England from 1811 to 1820, when George

III's madness meant that his eldest son, later George IV, ruled in his name. More broadly, books set between about 1800 and 1830 are usually considered Regency period." However, books set in England during this time period can be divided into two categories: Regencies and Regency historicals. The differences are important in terms of conducting readers' advisory. While some readers read both, a reader who asks for a Regency wants a Regency, not a Regency historical.

So what is the difference? Format, scope, length, focus, use of language. All of these. It is said best by Putney: "The traditional Regency traces its roots back to Jane Austen, and was brought to full flower by Georgette Heyer, whose wonderful, witty, beautifully written books are the foundation of the genre. In Georgette's world, there was no explicit sex, but there was wit and wisdom and a colorful picture of aristocratic society.

"Note that word 'society,' because it defines one of the key differences between the traditional Regency and the Regency historical. In many ways, the Regency is about society, while the historical is about passion. In a traditional Regency, one is always very aware of the limitations of society and the relationship must be resolved within those boundaries."

Currently, Zebra and Signet are the major publishers for the traditional Regency romance.

The Regency historical takes place during the same time period, but the plot often takes the characters away from society, or puts them at odds with it. The characters are probably in some way breaking the rules of society. For instance, the hero and heroine may be traveling together sans chaperone. There is a very good reason why this is so—usually a reason involving danger—and they both are fully aware that this will hopelessly compromise the heroine. However, because this is a romance, we know that in the end the hero will do the honorable thing and ask the heroine to marry him. A Regency historical will contain more adventure, more danger and buckling swash than the traditional Regency. The writing itself tends to be more intense and sensual. While in a traditional Regency romance there is no explicit sex, it can be very present in a Regency historical.

Inspirational Romance

Inspirational romances, according to Vince Brach, one of the founders of the Faith, Hope, and Love chapter of Romance Writers of America, represents about 6 percent of the total romance market. A fairly recent sub-genre, inspirationals as they are called, now have their own category in the RITA competition.

Under the Steeple Hill imprint, Silhouette has recently begun publishing a new line called Love Inspired. These are romances in which a nondenominational Christian element is as important as the relationship. In these books, emotional tenderness rather than sexual desire is stressed. Inspirational romances can be contemporary, historical, or even have paranormal elements to them.

While Steeple Hill books are mass-market-size paperbacks, other inspirationals are not. CBA—Christian Booksellers Association—affiliated publishers such as Tyndale House have put out trade-size paperback romances for several years. Some of these houses have an evangelical tone to their books and may require a statement of faith from the author.

Other publishers with inspirational romance lines include Word Publishing, WaterBrook, Palisades, Multnomah, and Barbour.

Romantic Suspense: Will He Kiss Me or Kill Me?

In a romantic suspense, both the elements of romance and suspense are fairly equal in importance. Both are necessary to the plot. A romantic suspense can be a category romance, such as Harlequin Intrigue, or it can be a single title. Readers who enjoy mysteries will often read a romantic suspense.

Many successful romance writers have broadened their readership by moving into romantic suspense, thereby attracting readers who would "never think of reading a romance." Tami Hoag, Anne Stuart, Eileen Dreyer, Karen Robards, and Nora Roberts have all written excellent romantic suspense.

The Paranormal: Witches and Ghosts and Vampires! Oh My!

A paranormal romance is one in which there is a paranormal element that is as much a part of the story as is the romance. There may be a vampire, or a ghost, or an angel. One of the characters may travel through time or be reincarnated. Romances that take place in the future or on distant planets are also usually included in this group.

I asked paranormal author Susan Krinard what she felt was the appeal of paranormal romances. She said, "The appeal of paranormal/fantasy romances lies, I think, in stretching the boundaries of imagination and escaping the 'real world.' The romantic element is still there, but set against a backdrop, or including characters, a little outside of 'reality.'"

Readers of paranormals are usually quite devoted to their subgenre. They will often comment that not enough of them are published. The publishers, on the other hand, usually say that the market for them is not there, that there aren't enough readers. Today, many fine paranormal romances, which were turned down by New York publishers, have been published electronically.

DIFFERENT TYPES OF PARANORMAL ROMANCES

Ghost	*Ghost of a Chance* by Casey Claybourne
	Ghosts by Antoinette Stockenberg
Fairy	*Fairytale* by Maggie Shayne
	Faery Magic (anthology) by Mary Jo Putney, Jo Beverley, Barbara Samuel, Karen Harbaugh
Reincarnation	*Every Time I Love You* by Heather Graham
	Body and Soul by Susan Krinard
Psychic	*The Bride Finder* by Susan Carroll
Time Travel	*The Reluctant Viking* by Sandra Hill

Angels	*Almost an Angel* by Deb Stover
	Daniel's Gift by Barbara Freethy
Genie	*Wishes Come True* by Kathleen Nance
Vampire	*The Vampire Viscount* by Karen Harbaugh
Werewolves	*Prince of Shadows* by Susan Krinard
Witch	*Bewitching* by Jill Barnett
Other Planets	*The White Sun* by Stobie Piel
	Lord of the Storm by Justine Davis

A Word about Anthologies

In the romance world, an anthology is a group of novellas—usually four—that have a common theme. Sometimes the theme is a holiday or something seasonal; sometimes it's an element in the story. I have written Christmas novellas for two anthologies, one having dogs as the common theme, the other magic. There have been anthologies about Mother's Day, about Elvis, about ghosts.

Readers tend to be aware of novellas written by their favorite authors and ask for them. When ordering romances, do not pass over anthologies.

Never Judge a Book by Its Cover

We librarians, of all people, should know and believe this. Yet it is by their covers, the thing that authors have the least control over, that romances are so often judged. Writers, unless they have big names, usually have no say about the cover of their books. We are given an art fact sheet to fill out and send in—descriptions of the main characters, the plot, any scenes that we think would make an interesting picture, any item that is significant in the story. Then we wait. We always hope to have a "good" cover, because a cover is the first thing a customer sees.

There is, historically, a reason for the "clench" cover. When the romance industry began to boom, corporate bookstore buyers were usually men. It didn't take the marketing people too long to discover that the corporate buyers were more likely to buy the books that had a scantily clad woman on the cover. Thus, the boom of bosoms.

Cover art, though, evolves. For a while, there were romances that had scantily clad men on the covers; after all, these were books for women. Several publishers have moved away from people on the covers in favor of flowers or step-backs, where, for instance, a floral cover opens up onto a secondary cover where there is a clench. Avon is currently doing humorous cut-paper designs on some of their covers, and some publishers are coming up with computer-generated graphics instead of using artists.

What do covers tell us about what's inside the pages? Quite a lot, if we choose to look. Savvy category readers recognize each line by its distinctive look. Harlequin Superromance covers look nothing like Silhouette Desires. The artwork on a Desire is surrounded by a deep red border, is usually provocative, and is always sensual. The artwork on Supers tends to be more open and inclusive, often with sky in the background. Silhouette Romances show people who look just plain happy, while characters on Intrigue covers are often looking over their shoulder in fear. The colors used in a Silhouette Romance are often bright and cheerful, while the colors used on an Intrigue are often darker and more foreboding. These are deliberate choices on the part of the art departments.

Covers for traditional Regency romances usually show a couple standing close together. Perhaps the man's arm is around the woman; however, this is not a clench. All pertinent body parts are demurely covered. Neither the man nor the woman is the slightest bit disheveled. Their smiles are pleasant and full of secret humor rather than smoldering passion. Regency historicals, on the other hand, can have cover art that is full of movement, is sensual, shows skin.

Artwork on a single title contemporary cover might be abstract. If it's a glamour and glitz novel, the artwork may have metallic ink. A medieval romance cover will most likely have a castle or the glove of a knight or a sword. If it takes place in Scotland, there will probably be a sprig of thistle. If it's a Western, there will probably be a cowboy hat or a gun or a pair of spurs. If there's a baby in the story, that baby will probably be on the cover. These are not clichés, but icons designed by the art department to catch the eye of readers who are looking for a particular kind of book. Most of my covers have had dogs on them. (I once had a letter from a reader who bought a copy of my book *Lonely Hearts* because the poodle on the cover looked exactly like her poodle.)

What does tend to be clichéd is the clench. Among readers there is no unanimous opinion about the clench cover. Some readers love them; some readers hate them. Some readers are embarrassed by them and cover them up with those fabric book covers. Sometimes readers and writers look at them and wonder how two humans can possibly contort their bodies into those positions. Certainly they must be mighty uncomfortable. The uncomfortable-looking clench cover is, of course, the origin of one of the pejorative term for romances, "bent neck."

A Word about Those Titles

A word about titles. Writers often do not choose their own titles. I have been lucky. Out of my five titles so far, three of them—*Stray Hearts, The Shepherds and Mr. Weisman,* and *Romeo and Julia*—have been my own. For my first Christmas novella, my editor asked me to come up with five Christmasy-sounding titles. My story takes place in an animal shelter on Christmas Eve, so right off the top of my head, I said "Away in a Shelter." And because I had just done story time at the library and was feeling silly, I added "Bark, the Hairy Angels Sing" and "While Shepherds Watched Their Dogs by Night." She said she'd get back to me. A couple of days later, she called me back and told me my story would be called *Away in a Shelter.*

I recently sat down with a stack of *Romantic Times* and looked at the different types of titles that came from different types of romances. Often the historicals had words such as *defiant,* and *warrior,* and *passion* in their titles, while the contemporaries, both category and single title, often had fun with a title: *What a Man's Got to Do,* and *A Cowboy Comes a'Courting,* and *Truly Madly Yours.*

2

Romance Writers

Not a Pink Boa in Sight

In 1998, there were 1,963 original and reprinted romance titles published. They were written by 1,196 authors.

When we think of a romance writer, we often imagine a pink-haired woman with a matching feather boa, a slinky gown with spaghetti straps and sequins, and a secretary to take down every silver word that she utters. Yes, this is the stereotype. And it is as valid as is the stereotype of the little-old-lady librarian with sensible shoes and hair in a bun. Except for maybe the sensible shoes part, neither stereotype is a true picture. Stereotypes never are. So what is the reality of a romance author?

Before writing romances full time, Justine Davis was a police officer. She saw a lot of unhappiness and misery in her work. Writing romances was for her a way of balancing the scales, bringing happily-ever-after endings into a world where there are precious few of them.

Romance author Stephanie Mittman says, "I do what writers have always done. I take words and string them together until they have the power and the grace to take a reader away. Being a historical writer, I take them to farms in the Midwest at the turn of the century, or to the Wild West of outlaws and heroes. But wherever

I set them, they all wind up in the same place . . . paradise. And if I've done it right, the reader winds up with a satisfied smile, clutching my book to her chest and sighing. There aren't a great many jobs you can do that leave your patrons, your consumers, your patients or clients, so content that they write you letters of gratitude. And I don't even have to get dressed or comb my hair to do it!"

Romance writers are intelligent people. Many of us have at least one college degree, and Ph.Ds are not unusual. Most of us are women, but there are a few men who write romances, usually under a female pseudonym. Many of us started out—and some have stayed—in professions other than writing:

Laura Kinsale—petroleum geologist

Judith Arnold—playwright

Elizabeth Bevarly—retail manager

Robin Burcell, Lynda Sandoval, Justine Davis/Justine Dare—
    police officers

Debra Dixon—business consultant

Kathleen Eagle, Susan Wiggs, Mary Balogh—teachers

Suzanne Forster—clinical psychologist

Tess Gerritson, Jeannie Brewer—physicians

Leigh Greenwood—choir director

Kristin Hannah—entertainment lawyer

Sally Tyler Hayes, Patricia Potter—journalists

Karen Leabo, Janet Lynnford—textbook editors

Merline Lovelace—Colonel, U.S. Air Force (retired)

Victoria Alexander—television news reporter

Teresa Medeiros—registered nurse

Joyce Sullivan—private investigator

Lorna Michaels—speech pathologist

Kathleen Nance—doctor of pharmacy

Joan Overfield—911 operator

Tori Phillips—historical re-enactor

Patricia Rice—certified public accountant

Linda Markowiak—attorney in the county prosecutor's office

Kathleen Korbel/Eileen Dreyer, Laurie Grant—emergency room nurses

Laurie Paige—systems analyst for NASA's Apollo missions

Susan Johnson—art historian

Susan Grant—commercial pilot

Julie Tetel—English professor

There are several writers who are or were librarians:

Annie Kimberlin

Cathie Linz

Deborah Shelley

Evelyn Richardson

Evelyn Rogers

Elizabeth DeLancey

Jayne Ann Krentz / Amanda Quick

Jo Manning

Lynn Lockhart

Pamela Morsi

Sally Hawkes

Sandra Kitt

Those of us who have chosen to write romances often feel the need to defend our chosen genre—and it is chosen. We write romances because we love it and because we believe in it. What could possibly be more fascinating than the interaction between two people in the throes of falling in love?

One of the questions romance writers are asked over and over is, "But when are you going to write a *real* book?" When Jennifer Greene, member of RWA's Hall of Fame, was in college, she realized that what she wanted to do with her life was to help women become empowered. She wanted women to know that they had choices in their lives. This is why she writes romances. Greene is one of the category writers who have pushed the envelope by writing romances about heroines who face such challenges as date rape, alcoholism, and drug addiction. Though not every book of Greene's is issue-oriented, every one of them is about a woman making a conscious choice about her life. Greene's books have been translated into more than twenty-five different languages and have sold many million copies all over the world. She writes *real* books.

Another question often asked of romance writers is, "Can I help you with your research?" (usually asked by a sleazy-looking man sporting a great big leer). A variation of this is, "I bet you just write about it cause you don't get enough at home." This kind of comment is both offensive and absurd. It is also more common than anyone could possibly imagine.

"How long does it take you to churn out one of those babies? A weekend or two?" This is actually an interesting question. It depends on the individual writer and the individual book. Some writers write quickly, some slowly. Some of us—I'm in this category—write in fits and starts, along with working at a day job. Some writers write one book a year; others write two or three or more. Some books require more research than others. There is no set answer. This is not, after all, a matter of downloading a romance book template and filling in the pertinent names and hair colors.

As already stated, in 1998, there were 1,963 original and reprinted romances published, written by 1,196 authors. Libby Hall, in the June issue of the *Romance Writers' Report,* the journal of the Romance Writers of America, writes, "Of the 1,196 authors, 803 had one book out, 260 had two books, 86 had three, 41 had four, 14 had five, 8 had six, 6 had seven while 3 had eight titles, 2 had eleven and–ta-da—Marie Ferrerella set a new record with 12 original titles out in 1998." However, it's always important to remember that even though an author may have several books published in a particular year, all may not have been written within one year.

My personal favorite comment of this type is, "Yeah, I'm gonna write a book someday. As soon as I get some free time." Writing a book cannot be done in "free time." It is a process that consumes every moment of a writer's life. We drive down the street listening to our characters carry on a conversation. We stand in line at the grocery store pondering motivation. Stories, plots, bits of scenes are continually simmering in the backs of our minds.

By Any Other Name:
A Word about Pseudonyms

Today the use of a pseudonym is usually the decision of the author. Personally, I chose a pseudonym because my last name, Bouricius, is not pronounced the way it looks and is not spelled the way it sounds, and I've gotten so many variations of it over the years that I decided to make it easy for my readers. I chose Kimberlin, a name from my mother's family tree, and now write romances under the name Annie Kimberlin.

On the other hand, Linda Markowiak, who writes for Harlequin Superromance, writes under her own name. She says she likes her Polish name and wanted it on her books. Besides, she decided the world was ready for more ethnic names on books.

Alice Duncan, however, writes under several different pseudonyms for several different publishers. She started out writing for Harper as Alice Duncan, which is her real name. Then, under the name Rachel Wilson, she wrote for Berkley/Jove, who told her they liked authors to have a name associated solely with their company. Dell wanted her to write for them as Alice Duncan, but didn't want her to use that name elsewhere at the same time she was with them, so when she sold a book to Leisure, she took the name Emma Craig. Duncan has recently written two books for the Trailsman series of genre Westerns under the name Jon Sharpe—the author-name for that series. Though this sounds quite convoluted, Duncan has a terrific sense of humor about it all. She says she writes a lot and this is one way to keep her books in the stores. Besides, she adds, she's not proud. She'll do anything to keep away from a day job.

Victoria Alexander was a television reporter when she began writing romances. She decided to use a pseudonym for her books because she didn't want her viewers to wonder, "She makes up stories; will she report accurately?" She used the names of her children to create her pseudonym, but she still uses her real name when doing work in other media.

Some authors choose different names for different types of books. For instance, Eileen Dreyer writes medical thrillers under her own name, while continuing to write deeply moving category romances for Silhouette under the name Kathleen Korbel. Likewise, Sue Civil-Brown recently began writing single title contemporaries under her own name while writing her Conard County books for Silhouette under the name Rachel Lee.

We librarians need to be sure to include cross-references in our catalogs for romance writers, just as we do for Stephen King. This is a matter of accuracy and of providing our patrons with complete information. Where do we find all these names? In *Romantic Times,* on romance Web sites, or on author sites, to name just a few places. Check appendix H for a list of some writers who write under two or more names.

3

Readers of Romance

A Box of Bon-Bons, a Good Romance, and Thou

Romance Readers Are Loyal

Romance readers are an incredibly loyal lot. Several years ago a woman came up to the information desk at my branch. She'd read everything Rosanne Bittner had ever written and was devastated because she had to wait for several months before a new book was due out. She wanted to write to Bittner but didn't know how to do so. This was in the days before the Internet and e-mail and Web site were common in our library, so I looked up the address of Bittner's publisher. Then I also looked through the previous year's *Romantic Times (RT)*. In every issue, *RT* has several author spotlights and often they include an address for writing to that author.

Today, when looking for a romance author's address, I use several sources. For Web addresses I often go to the Romance Writers of America site, rwanational.com, where there is a link to a listing of homepages of many romance authors. I also use search engines to track down author homepages. Most publishers have a section on their homepages where they feature their authors, and sometimes there are links to individual homepages. I have also been known to thumb through past *RTs*. Many authors send out postcards or announcements when they have a new book coming out. On their homepage is usually an address, either e- or snail mail, if a reader wants to be put on the mailing list. Incidentally, it's considered courteous to send a self-addressed stamped envelope (SASE) if the reader would like a reply.

Readers want to write to authors because romances are about deep emotional experiences. When a writer has touched their lives deeply, readers often need to touch that writer's life as well. Sometimes readers want to tell a writer what their books meant to them. Sometimes readers write to an author to correct a piece of information in a book. Readers write to me and sometimes send me pictures of their dogs and cats, which I post on a bulletin board above my computer.

Romance authors love to hear from readers and treasure their letters. Writing is a solitary activity. At the library I get lots of feedback from patrons. Kids come up to the desk and tell me they really liked the book I gave them last week, and would I suggest another just like it. Patrons are thrilled when we find that recipe for bourbon chicken or for ranger cookies, and they tell us so. But writing is different. We put much of ourselves in our books and then send them off into the world. Quite frankly, when I send off a book to my agent, I always feel the same way I did when I sent my kids off on the first day of kindergarten. Excited for them, yes, but also nervous and scared. The only difference is that when I send a book off, I don't cry. When someone sends me a letter and tells me that they've loved my books, I know I've "done good." Suddenly, all the missed dinners, the late nights at the computer, the times I couldn't go to the movies are all worth it. So when I find a patron who has loved a particular book, no matter what that book is, I often suggest they write to that author.

Stephanie Mittman once received a letter from a woman who said, "I have read your book twice in two weeks and plan on reading it at least four or five more times. I feel as if the characters in the book have become my friends . . . I have a feeling of sadness that by closing the pages I am losing friends." Another woman wrote to Mittman after reading her book *Angels in the Snow.* "Graham and Francie Trent [characters in *Angels in the Snow*] will always live in my memory, a memory until now clouded with misery and pain. When I think of wedding nights, their beautiful one, not my own, will be remembered. My wedding night was legal rape and theirs was such a contrast. I cannot tell you what Graham and Francie mean to me. Thank you for penning such a love story. I will always treasure it." Mittman says she often receives letters telling her how she took a reader away from her troubles for just a few hours and gave her a good laugh or a good cry.

One young reader wrote to Sue Krinard, "I am fifteen years old. About two years ago I bought your book *Prince of Shadows*. I love that book so much. . . . It inspired me to become a wolf biologist."

That's right. A letter from a teenager. Yes, teenagers also read romance. In fact, many romance readers began reading romances when they were teenagers. According to a market research study conducted by BBC Research and Consulting, Inc., 43 percent "of romance readers report that they discovered romance novels before their fifteenth birthday" (*Romance Writers' Report*, Dec. 1999, p. 17). Some of them started reading their mothers' romances; some of them found romances on their own. One such woman said of her early reading that she wanted to know what it felt like to make love. She wanted not just the mechanics of it, but an understanding of the emotions involved. She knew that as a young teenager she wasn't ready to make love herself, but she wanted to know about it. In romances she found the answers to her questions. She also found stories that made her feel good about being a woman. She is a romance reader to this day.

Romance Readers and Proud

Jayne Ann Krentz begins the introduction to *Dangerous Men and Adventurous Women* by saying, "Few people realize how much courage it takes for a woman to open a romance novel on an airplane. She knows what everyone around her will think about both her and her choice of reading material." This was published almost ten years ago and times have not changed. Though perhaps more women now read romances in public, the stigma is still there. Not only are the books still seen as trash, but the women who read them are still seen as not quite bright. If we know the reader to be intelligent, we wonder what has possibly possessed her to make her read such mindless drivel. I have heard more than one librarian say such a thing.

We still persist in the stereotypical belief that women who read romances can't get a date on Friday night. Instead, they lounge around all day eating bon-bons while they read their little books. This is simply untrue.

The Romance Writers of America Web site has some statistics about romance readers:

> An estimated forty-five million women in North America read romance novels.
>
> Romance readers range in age from fifteen to 105.
>
> 68 percent of romance readers attended or graduated from college.
>
> 55 percent of romance readers work outside the home and maintain an average household income of $45,300 per year.
>
> 48 percent of romance readers began reading romances when they were seventeen or younger.
>
> Women with full-time, executive-level jobs report reading an average of fourteen romances per month.

Carol Vantresca is a committed romance reader. She also has a Ph.D. in sociology and works for the Ohio State University's Office of Continuing Education. Vantresca began reading romances several years ago during a particularly stressful period in her life. Someone gave her romances to help her relax and fall asleep at night. Instead, she says, they kept her up reading. "But they were good for my blood pressure," she adds with a laugh. She's been reading romances ever since. She reads romances for pure escapism and for the wonderful writing and for the happily-ever-after ending.

Vantresca says she reads romances by author, rather than by setting or subject. When she finds an author whose voice she particularly likes, she wants to read all her other books. When Vantresca first started reading romances, she would go to the library with a list of works by a particular author and perhaps find only two. At that time romances in her local library weren't cataloged, so there was little a librarian could do to help her find what she needed, even if she'd been comfortable enough to ask for assistance. This was at a time when she was still hiding the covers. Now she doesn't care what other people think of her reading romances. "I like them," she says.

What would she like librarians to know about romance readers? "We're highly intelligent people," she says, "who have purposely chosen to read romance because we love it." She adds that librarians should encourage reading rather than discouraging it. Libraries need to make sure that their librarians are open enough to learn about genre fiction, read genre fiction, and are willing to advocate genre fiction.

Another romance reader, Ann Taylor, used to think romances were simple-minded books, written at a low reading level. She had the impression that they were all interchangeable, except for the names of the characters. Then one day, her friend, who was an enthusiastic librarian—yours truly—talked her into reading one. She read it and was hooked. She found romances weren't at all what she'd thought. They were interesting and well written. And they had strong women.

Before she retired, Taylor was a lieutenant colonel with the Air National Guard. When she was called up to active duty during Operation Desert Storm, she made sure she took a stack of romances with her. Once in Saudi Arabia, she read romances while she was waiting "for things to get started," and then later at night to relax.

Taylor was a navigator, and during her years in the service, flew all over the world. On one trip, the pilot started teasing her about the studly hunk on the cover of her current romance novel. He joked that of course the hero of the book had to be some god named Thor who had a huge sword, *wink, wink.* From then on, the rest of the crew, who were all men, jokingly referred to her romances as "Ann's Thor books."

But wait, you say, why are these obviously intelligent women reading romances? Because they want a book that leaves them feeling hopeful about the world. They want a book in which the woman struggles and wins, a book that reaffirms all the good things about life. Trust me, if I were flying a jet over a war zone all day, when I got into bed at night, I sure wouldn't want to read about serial killers.

Not all romance readers are women. There are men who read romances. Yes, by choice. Granted, there are not many of them, at least not many who will admit to it. But read them they do. And for the same reasons that women read romance, because they enjoy a great story and a happy ending. According to a market research study conducted by BBC Research and Consulting, Inc., three and a half million men read romances—about 9 percent of all romance readers (*Romance Writers' Report*, Dec. 1999, p. 27).

John Charles, a librarian in Arizona, began reading romances about twenty years ago. John had been a "mysteries only" reader until one day when he was shelving fiction. He picked up a copy of *The Seventh Sinner* by Elizabeth Peters to put on the shelf when the cover caught his attention. He read the inside jacket copy and was hooked. He read every book that he could find by Elizabeth Peters, and then Barbara Michaels, and on to Victoria Holt and Phyllis Whitney. From there he moved on to Regencies and eventually contemporary romances. John says he got a bit of kidding when he first started reading romances, but this was when he was less secure about what he liked to read. Now he doesn't care what other people think of his reading choices.

Vince Brach, who has a Ph.D. in biology and teaches high school sciences, also was hooked by chance. Snowbound in Dallas over a weekend, he picked up a romance. He was hooked and began to read widely in the genre. Brach had already published magazine articles, so it became an obvious thing for him to write a romance as well. Does he get flak about reading romances and writing them? Occasionally. Usually from men. But he says his "self-image does not require stereotypical reinforcement from either sex." However, when he published his first romance, he did use a pseudonym—Fran Vincent—suggested by his wife. He says, "IMHO [in my humble opinion] a man writing romance under his own name (assuming the publisher would allow it) is a fool—he'll guarantee his own failure. Many women do not believe that men are capable of experiencing or expressing 'real' love, much less putting a credible love story together. It's tough enough getting a readership today without having to fight the sex prejudice battle."

Can reading romances help men understand what women really want? According to Colin McEnroe, the answer is yes. In his highly humorous and on-target article "Unleash Your Inner Fabio," he tells men, "Somebody spends roughly $750 million every year on romance novels, and it probably isn't you and Reggie White and Bruce Willis. The woman you love right now or the next woman you meet may be getting a lot of her ideas about men, love, and sex from romance novels. I mean, if you were going up against the Jets next week, wouldn't you like a peek at Parcells' playbook?" (*Men's Health,* Sept. 1998, p. 90)

A True Story about a Librarian, a Stroke Survivor, and a Romance

Several years ago I was working the evening shift at the information desk on an unusually slow night. An elderly gentleman came up to the desk for assistance. His speech was fairly garbled and I had to concentrate to understand what he was saying. However, I finally figured out what he needed and found the information for him. He apologized for his speech. He said he'd had a stroke and was learning to speak all over again. "How interesting," I told him. I'd just finished reading a book that took place in the early 1800s about a man who had a stroke. But the doctors then didn't know what a stroke was and they thought he was insane. So they put him in a mental institution. I told my gentleman patron that in the book, when the man was able to speak again, the first things he could spit out were swear words. My patron nodded. Yes, that had happened to him as well, and it had greatly distressed his wife who was not used to such language. Then my patron asked me what the book was. I told him it was *Flowers from the Storm,* a romance by a woman named Laura Kinsale. He said he'd like to read it, so I ran over to the romance section and grabbed up the last copy on our shelves.

A few weeks later, my gentleman patron came back to the library to see me. He said he'd read Kinsale's book and then, because it seemed to describe so perfectly what he'd gone through, he gave it to his wife to read. Then he gave it to his doctor. The doctor read it also and said that he'd recommend it to the families of his stroke patients to help them better understand the recovery process of their loved ones.

The moral of this story? Don't underestimate the power of romance for your patrons.

4

Romance v. "Real" Books

The Controversy Lives On

$\mathscr{T}$he sufferance of popular literature in libraries is not a new issue. It has been debated since at least the mid-1800s. The June 15, 1996, issue of *Library Journal* contains a piece by George Watson Cole originally published in 1884 that is a "plea for the masses." In it, Cole points out that "the library is in existence by the grace of the public, and it is its duty to cater to *all* the classes that go towards making up the community in which it is established." Cole goes on to quote an article on this same issue by F. B. Perkins published in 1876. This discussion has been going on for one and a quarter centuries and we still haven't gotten it right.

When I was in library school, we once had a discussion about the merits, or lack of them, of allowing (note the word "allow") romances in public libraries. It was a heated discussion. Most of us, being young and idealistic and having no practical experience in libraries, seemed to feel that romances didn't belong there. After all, libraries were for quality literature. Real books. We didn't seem to remember that Dickens and Shakespeare wrote the popular literature of their day. So did the Brontës and Mary Shelley. Let's not forget Chaucer. Perhaps in one hundred years, the romances of today will be considered literature. Perhaps we'll even have *Cliff's Notes* on romances: a discussion of theme and characterization and plot points, and use of point of view.

A Four-Step Program

Librarians have traditionally had an uneasy relationship with romances. The romances are willing, but the librarians seem unsure. Still, there seems to be a sort of continuum for libraries on their progression toward enlightenment regarding their treatment of the romance genre. I first described this progression in an article I coauthored with Cathie Linz and Carole Byrnes that was published in the May/June 1995 issue of *Public Libraries*. That progression, with tongue planted firmly in cheek, goes something like this:

Step 1

Libraries are the keepers of quality literature. Therefore bodice busters (the term is always said with a slight sneer) are consigned to a take-one-leave-one box out in the lobby. The books are there on sufferance. The library makes no attempt to claim them, and statistics are not kept. Books rotate purely by chance.

Step 2

The romances move inside the library. Perhaps a shelf or two are located somewhere to keep them inside but out of sight; we don't, after all, wish to offend our real patrons. The books, mostly donated, rarely purchased, are stamped with the library's name, but the library does not catalog them. Circulation statistics may be kept manually, by hash marks. Neither patrons nor library staff knows what is owned, and the professional staff doesn't particularly care to know. Weeding is by natural causes; the books are not returned. Sometimes they show up at local garage sales.

Step 3

The books are bar-coded and linked to a generic record that probably reads "paperback romance." When a patron calls to ask the title of that book that is overdue, the circulation clerk can only say it's a paperback romance. (Doesn't matter what the title is because those books're all alike, don'tcha know.) The records are generic, so there is no way the staff and patrons know what books are owned. Any readers' advisory is purely by luck. Acquisition is still by donation, though there may be some deliberate attempt to purchase titles by more respected romance authors such as Nora Roberts. Her books are probably cataloged and shelved with the general fiction.

Step 4

At some point in time, the library will notice that the circulation figures for these "paperback romances" are high. The library will eventually realize the wisdom of giving each book its own catalog record instead of the generic one. This means the readers and library staff will know what is owned, and reserves can be placed. This means that readers will expect the library to own certain titles, which in turn means that someone on the staff will have to be responsible for—*gasp*—ordering the things.

Why Collection Development by Donation Is Not a Good Thing

Collection development by donation is haphazard at best, wholly inadequate at worst. It is dependent on the kindness of readers. Readers do not generally donate the books they like best, their keepers. Instead, they donate the books they don't want to keep. This is a no-brainer. Also, people usually donate their books right before they move, or when they're cleaning out their basement, or before the end of the year for tax purposes. Because of this, donations are often old and yellowed; many are well thumbed. Serious, rather than casual, romance readers usually have the broadest collections, and when they weed, they usually find a used bookstore with which they can trade. Often they trade with each other. Consequently, the library that depends on donations will not have a very broad or current selection to offer their patrons. Certainly there will be no depth. What is a librarian to do?

Simply this. Go about selecting, ordering, cataloging, processing, and suggesting romances as you would titles in any other genre. With knowledge and careful forethought.

Selection? Several years ago I knew a librarian who ordered by marking every third romance title in the *Ingram's Paperback Advance*. Since this was before my own conversion, I didn't think anything of it at the time. However, I have often wished I could go back in time and test her collection just to see how the law of averages came into play. I am, after all, the daughter of a scientist.

Librarians who select materials for purchase usually do so with much thought. We read review sources, we read author interviews, we keep our ears cocked when we watch the morning news. And we listen to our patrons. We also know what we own, what circulates, and what we need more and less of. We do not take collection development lightly. After all, we are responsible for the spending of tax dollars.

When we develop and maintain our romance collection, we must use the same standards we use when working with the rest of our collection. To do less is to cheat the taxpayer and also the romance reading patron.

"But wait," you say, "romances are not reviewed." Au contraire, cherie. This may have been true once upon a time, but true

---

PROFESSIONAL REVIEW SOURCES FOR ROMANCE

| *Library Journal* | *Booklist* | *Publishers Weekly* |

NONTRADITIONAL REVIEW SOURCES FOR ROMANCE

| *Affaire de Coeur* | *Rendezvous* | *Romantic Times* |

ONLINE REVIEW SOURCES FOR ROMANCE

| Under the Covers | The Book Nook | Genreflecting |

it is no longer. There are both traditional and nontraditional sources for romance reviews.

Several professional journals now review romances. *Library Journal* has a romance roundup four times a year. *Publishers Weekly* often includes a romance or two in its Mass Market section. And *Booklist* began in September 1998 reviewing romances in every issue. Still, this is a small percentage of reviews for the huge number of romances that are published each month.

BookPage has a romance column in each issue, and several major newspapers are beginning to review romances. But probably the greatest number of romance reviews can be found in *Romantic Times (RT)*. It is a fan magazine aimed at readers, and the reviews reflect this. *RT*'s reviews tend to be more descriptive than evaluative. Single titles are given more review space than category romances, which only receive two or three sentences. The number rating system is controversial among readers and writers, and the emphasis on cover models tends to weaken the credibility of the genre among professionals. All these things are true. But I repeat: This is a fan magazine. Still, librarians who want to see the broad spectrum of new books for the month would be well advised to read *RT*. It has other features, such as interviews with authors, agents, and publishers, which make it valuable to a romance-friendly librarian.

Affaire de Coeur is another review source for romances. It also includes articles of interest on the genre. Though it doesn't include as many reviews as *RT,* it does give more space to category romances.

Rendezvous is a monthly review of romances, mysteries, and women's fiction. It's published by Love Designers Writer's Club, Inc. *Rendezvous* does not accept advertisements of any kind, and they give reviews for category romance as much space as reviews for single titles.

Online, Diana Tixier-Herald has a Web site for *Genreflecting* that includes romance reviews. Also, *Under the Covers* reviews many kinds of genre fiction and has a very strong romance section. Many online bookstores post reviews as well as readers' comments.

Today, there are many fan Web sites that post reviews of romances. While they may not be the sites librarians use to make purchasing decisions, they are very worth perusing to get a feel of what's being said about what books. When looking at a Web site, we need to use common sense and the same standards we use when evaluating any Web site: credibility, currency, quality, and so on. Always keep in mind the fact that most sites are focused on sharing books with readers. Look at the reviews carefully. Most, but not all, reviewers review because they love the genre, and because there is a certain thrill in reading a long-awaited book before it hits the stands. See appendixes 3 and 4 for a short list of credible Web sites.

To Catalog or Not to Catalog

This is a real no-brainer. Of course we should catalog romances. Furthermore, we should catalog romances with full records, and author searches should include references to other pseudonyms. Here is why.

There's simply no point in having a book if we don't know we have it and can't find it when we need it. We cannot serve our patrons this way. Isn't helping people find the information and books they need, after all, the reason we do what we do? "But wait," you say, "patrons at my library never ask for romances." Try to figure out why. I'll bet you anything that they're reading them. If we don't have our romances cataloged, then what good would it do for readers to ask us for them by title or author? Women who read romances are intelligent women. They know what barcodes mean. If we are not getting romance questions, then perhaps we should examine the way we treat the genre. To paraphrase the immortal line from Pogo, we have met the snob, and he is us.

I have heard librarians say that they don't catalog their romances because they are not hardbound and so don't last long enough to make it worth it. In my branch there are some paperback romances that have circulated forty-eight times and are still in decent shape. There are also brand-new hardbound books that have circulated once and fallen apart. If you are truly concerned about your paperback romances looking shabby, invest in some clear book tape and reinforce the spines of the new books when they come in. (This is, by the way, an excellent job for volunteers.) Why do romances look so shabby after a while? Because they're read. They're small enough to fit in a purse and they go with women to the orthodontist's office, to the playground at the fast food place, to the swimming pool. Wherever women go, romances go too.

Another reason to catalog romances is because they are good for circulation statistics. My library system runs a stock turnover report every year. There are divisions for different Dewey areas, for nonbook media by type, and for various fiction genres. Over the last couple of years, I have kept an eye on the statistics for romance paperbacks. The stock turnover rate for romance is consistently three or four times higher than westerns and science fiction/fantasy, and about twice as high as mysteries. I've also checked the stock turnover rates for some of the other branches in my system and find the same general numbers. Interestingly enough, these numbers are similar to the sales figures for romance as compared with other genres. So by not cataloging our romances we are not getting accurate circulation statistics.

How should they be cataloged? In an ideal world, romances would have full records that are searchable by author, title, series title, and category line including number. The MARC record would include notations of any prequels, in order. Various pseudonyms would be cross-referenced. Subject headings would be used.

However, ideal worlds are the worlds of romance novels. We have to live in the real one. In practical terms, the bare minimum requirements for catalog access to romances are author and title, with cross-references for any additional pseudonyms.

Many libraries use genre labels to identify genres such as mysteries, westerns, science fiction, and romance. If you interfile your genres with your general fiction, brightly colored labels on the spines will help readers find them. If you separate out your genres, they will be easier for the pages to identify and shelve in the correct section. (Labeling genre fiction is another good job for volunteers.)

But Where Shall We Put Them?

If Dewey were to classify romances, he might first identify the genre as a whole, then he would begin by breaking them down into major divisions. For this is, after all, how many readers describe their romances. The first division would be between contemporary and historical romances, with a third division for books we shall call for the time being "other." Then each of these divisions would be further divided. In fact, a Dewey-type classification system might look something like this:

```
100   Contemporary Romance
      110   Single Title
120   Series
      121   Harlequin
            121.1   Harlequin Romance
            121.2   Harlequin Presents
            121.3   Harlequin Superromance
            Etc.
      122   Silhouette
            122.1   Silhouette Romance
            122.2   Silhouette Desire
            122.3   Silhouette Special Edition
            Etc.
200   Historical
      210   Prehistory to 1000
      220   Medieval 1000-1500
            220.914    England
            220.9144   Scotland
      230   1500-1800
            230.914    England
            230.915    Scotland
            230.973    United States
            230.999    Any other location
```

Of course, if we truly followed Dewey's scheme, the 200s would be reserved for inspirational romances, and the time travels would probably be classed in the 629s. Historical romances would be in the 900s, and my books, which all feature strong dog characters, would probably be in the 636.7s.

Tongue-in-cheek aside, how we shelve romances is an issue worth our thought. The way we treat a genre gives a message to the readers of that genre. If we treat the books as if they are not important, then we are telling a group of our patrons that what they read is of little consequence.

So what do we do with romances? This is one of those times when we are called upon to be creative. What works for one library may not work for another. There are as many solutions as there are concerned librarians. Some libraries separate all their genre fiction, some only separate paperbacks. Each library must come up with its own solution, based on its own limitations and the scope of its collection. However, there are some basic issues that should be thoughtfully considered when making a decision to separate romances.

Issue 1

Genre romances are published mainly in paperback. However, some authors—Amanda Quick, Kathleen Eagle, Mary Jo Putney, and Jennifer Crusie, just to name a few—are writing romances that are published in hardback. If we separate genres, what do we do with the hardbacks of those genres? Do we separate the paperback romances but treat the hardbacks as if they're general fiction? This means that the reader who is looking for Mary Jo Putney will have to be savvy enough to look in both the paperback romances and the general fiction. Likewise, the librarian. Yes, catalog entries should be complete enough to list exact location, so if the patron is looking in the catalog she will see that Putney's books are in both places. But the patron may not look in the catalog at all, especially if romances have not been traditionally cataloged in that library. She may go directly to the shelves where she has always found Putney's books and thereby miss some titles. And what happens when a hardback romance is released in paperback? Do we shelve it next to the hardback copy in the general fiction? Or with the paperback romances?

In my particular branch we have not come up with a good solution to this issue. However, for several years we have shelved hardback Westerns with the paperback Westerns. Same with mysteries, and with science fiction/fantasy.

Issue 2

Some libraries shelve their category romances by lines. For instance, the Silhouette Special Editions are over here, the Harlequin Temptations are over there, single title romances are over there, and so on. This is also how most bookstores shelve their romances. Some libraries then arrange them by author and some sequentially by their number. Because category romances all have a distinct look, this tends to look nice and neat, and librarians seem to like things nice and neat. However, looks can be deceiving. Patricia Potter has written for Harlequin Historicals, Loveswept, Silhouette, and Bantam. Some of her books are also out in hardcover. In order to find her books, we would have to look in several different places.

Some libraries dump all the paperback romances together on the shelf, loosely sorted by the first letter of the author's last name. This certainly makes it easy for the library pages. Caution. If we "dump" romances, we are telling romance readers that these authors and books are not important enough to alphabetize. Our snobbery is showing. Besides, when a patron asks me to help her find a book by Ann Tyler, I go to the shelves and pull it right off. However, when that same patron asks me to help her find a book by Stephanie Mittman, I go to the romance shelves and have to sort through all the Ms in order to find it. This looks tacky and unprofessional. It also takes more time. Not that I mind taking more time to find a particular book. After all, this gives me more time to do RA with that patron. While we're looking for the Mittman we'll run across books by Pamela Morsi. "Have you read *Simple Jess*?" I might ask. "If you like Mittman, you might try Morsi. Or Debbie Macomber." As a book pusher, I can be shameless.

Issue 3

What should we do with the inspirational romances? Do we keep them with the romances, or put them with the Christian fiction? Where will they best be found by the people who want to read them? According to Vince Brach, one of the founders of the Faith,

Hope, and Love chapter of Romance Writers of America, many readers of Christian fiction would be unlikely to browse a separate romance section, preferring instead to choose books they know will not offend their beliefs.

And what about romances by African-American authors? Do we keep them with the romances or put them in the African-American collection, as some bookstores do? Not all romances by African-American writers are about African-American characters.

Issue 4

Where do we physically put them? Do we put them in some out-of-sight place as if we're ashamed to have them in our library? As if they are an afterthought? Serious romance readers can become very defensive when they think their genre is not valued. This is something they've had a lot of experience with. Sometimes they make an issue of it, and sometimes they simply go away and find their books elsewhere. For a public library supposedly open to all, this is not a good thing. If we have ever made a patron feel unwelcome because of her reading choices, either passively or actively, then we ought to be very ashamed of ourselves.

Collection Maintenance

There is more to maintaining a collection than ordering and cataloging. We have to weed and replace. Weeding a romance collection can be a tricky thing. While we want to keep the things that are still being read, we also want to make room for the new titles that will be published. Remember that in 1998 there were almost 2,000 romance titles published. How do we make room for these new books on our shelves?

I've always secretly hated weeding fiction. Nonfiction is easy. It's easy to discard an out-of-date edition of a medical dictionary when the new edition arrives. It's easy to tell at a glance if a book hasn't circulated in a while or if the information is out of date. If it's still worth being in the collection and we think we can push it, we'll give it the benefit of the doubt. Sometimes we put up a display of wallflowers and call it "The Best of the Bottom Shelf" or something like that.

But the romances in my branch circulate so much it's not a matter of the books having a low circ count, but of their condition. Often, the most popular romances are the ones in the worst shape. Why? Because these are the books that are read over and over, so they are just plain worn out. They've gone on canoe trips and cruise ships. They've gone on picnics and to hockey practice. They've gone on car trips across the country and sailing on the Great Lakes. Some of them, in the case of my friend Ann Taylor, who took several romances to Saudi Arabia with her, have even been in a war. They have lived a more exciting life than I have.

When faced with a book truck of candidates for withdrawal, look at each book carefully. Check the age and condition of the book. Is it part of an ongoing series that is still being published? Is it by an author who is still publishing? Is this author still in demand? Is this book still in demand? Has it circulated within the limits of your guidelines? Is it an award winner? Is this book listed on one of the bookmarks you regularly give out to your patrons? Is it a book you or someone on your staff personally likes to push? If the answer to the majority of these questions is no, then you should probably discard it. "But, wait," you say, "isn't this the same way we weed our general fiction?" Yes. It is.

While weeding popular fiction is much like weeding general fiction, ordering replacements is another thing. By the time many titles need to be replaced they are out of print. This is especially true in the case of category romances. This may mean keeping a shabby but very much in demand book still on the shelves. It may mean sending that book to the bindery. One thing to remember is that just because a book is no longer carried by the major jobbers does not mean it cannot be ordered directly from the publisher. And keep in mind that some of the major online bookstores will do out-of-print title searches.

Romance readers like to read the new books. They often wait eagerly for a new book by their favorite author, have often read excerpts at the author's Web site, or in *RT*, or in an author's newsletter. In a popular collection, having a wide variety of new titles is crucial. However, when romance readers find an author they like, they also want to read all the previous titles by that author.

Should there be a set percentage of new-to-old romance titles in your collection? That's a matter for each library to determine. I do think, however, that the majority of a popular fiction collection should consist of books published within the last three or four years. The romance genre is continually evolving. For instance, the distant and domineering heroes who were so prevalent several years ago have disappeared. Most of the glamour and glitz novels of the early 1990s have also become passé, as have the "sweet savage" story lines. Librarians should make themselves aware of these changes and order accordingly. How does one learn of these changes? One place is Kristin Ramsdell's annual article on the romance genre in *What Do I Read Next?* (annual, Gale). The many online sites devoted to romance will also give librarians this kind of information.

So you're now reading reviews, ordering romances, cataloging them, shelving them appropriately, and maintaining the collection. What's next? Romance readers' advisory.

5

Romance Readers' Advisory

How to Be Romance-Reader Friendly

*T*here are a number of ways you can make your library romance-reader friendly.

If your library does not currently purchase romances, do so.

If your library does not currently catalog romances, do so.

If you do not read romances as you do mysteries, science fiction, and the latest book by James Patterson, do so.

Read the romance reviews in *Library Journal, Publishers Weekly,* and *Booklist.* Consider it a professional responsibility. It *is* a professional responsibility.

Many authors have newsletters they send to people on their mailing lists. You can find out about these newsletters from such places as individual author sites on the Internet, or from the author profiles in *Romantic Times.* Write to these authors and ask to be put on their mailing lists. Then keep a file of these newsletters for your romance readers.

Call romance publishers and ask to receive their catalogs.

Do passive readers' advisory by creating bookmarks with romance themes. Begin with some of the booklists in appendix G.

Attend a romance writers' or readers' conference. This is a professional growth opportunity.

If you have a book discussion group, read a romance. If you don't have a book discussion group, consider starting a Romance Readers Book Discussion Group.

Subscribe to and circulate *Romantic Times, Affaire de Coeur,* or *Rendezvous*. Post a sign in your romance section telling your readers where these magazines can be found. Or shelve the magazines with the romances.

At your checkout desk, keep a festive-looking basket filled with new romances for patrons to check out. Also, keep a basket of romances in your picture book area so mothers can read while their children browse.

At a Public Library Association genre-cluster workshop, Joyce Saricks, coauthor of *Readers' Advisory: Service in the Public Library,* 2nd ed. (American Library Association, 1997), suggested librarians keep a book truck filled with great reads in front of the reference desk. This way, people who are waiting in line for reference service can browse. If you do this, make sure romances are on that truck.

Create a bulletin board for genre readers to post minireviews of books they like.

Keep an updated list of award-winning romances at your reference desk. When the awards are announced, post a list of the winning titles in your romance section. Set up a display of the award winners.

Finalists for the RITA awards are usually announced on the Romance Writers of America (RWA) Web site in early April. Purchase multiple copies of all the titles and have them available for checkout. Invite readers to read them and cast their own votes. The winning books are announced midsummer at Romance Writers of America's national conference and posted on RWA's Web site. Amazon.com also lists RITA finalists and winners.

Keep up on the romance world by logging onto RWA's Web site and other online sources and by perusing *Romantic Times, Affaire de Coeur,* and *Rendezvous.*

Encourage your state library association to include workshops on the romance genre in their annual conferences. Invite local romance writers to speak.

Encourage your library to hold a system-wide seminar on the romance genre.

If you attend the American Library Association or Public Library Association conferences, stop at the RWA booth and say hello.

Sponsor a Romance Reading Program. Begin in January. Every time a patron reads a romance she can put her name in a jar. Draw a name on Valentine's Day. Ask a local restaurant to donate a dinner for two.

If you're a secret romance reader, as I was for several years, gather up your courage and read romances in public. It's liberating.

Write to Romance Writers of America and request a *Look Who's Reading Romance* poster to use in displays. Also, log onto their Web site and sign up for their free newsletter for librarians and booksellers. Librarians can become associate members of RWA.

When someone comes up to the information desk and asks for the newest book by Nora Roberts and it's checked out—do some readers' advisory and, if it's appropriate, suggest a romance by another author.

And the next time you hear anyone say anything pejorative about a "bodice buster," set them straight.

How Much Sex Do You Like?

Readers' advisory is an important aspect of our jobs. Sometimes it appears in an obvious way. "Do you have any good books to read?" But sometimes it's subtler, almost sneaky. Anyone who's worked at an information desk knows that people don't always ask for what they really want. It could be that they're embarrassed to admit they read romances. Maybe in the past they've had an uncomfortable experience asking for romances. Perhaps the librarian on the desk is a man.

When someone asks me for a book by a particular author, I talk to her on the way to the shelves. I ask about that particular author and, based on what the reader says, I suggest other authors the reader might enjoy. If it's an author I'm not familiar with, I pay close attention. I am always on the lookout for a good book, a new author. If my reader asks for a particular title, our copy is checked out, and I have to place a reserve, I often suggest another book that she might like just so she has something to read while she's waiting for her book to arrive. If she asks me for "a good book to read," I ask her what kinds of things she's read before that she's liked, what she liked about them, and what kind of book she is in the mood for. Is there anything in particular that she doesn't want? This is not new. This is something we should all be doing automatically. This is a professional responsibility. This is what makes us book-pushing professionals.

If, based on the reader's answers to my questions, I feel a romance is appropriate, I suggest one. Or two. If a reader says she likes Robin Cook, I suggest Eileen Dreyer or Tess Gerritson. Then I tell them that Dreyer was an emergency room nurse and Gerritson was a physician, and that they both began their writing careers writing romances. Check appendix B for a list of suggested read-alikes. There are other lists in the appendixes as well. However, remember that these lists are simply suggestions and are not written in permanent ink. I see a list as a stepping stone to start you off, not a final stop. You must continue adding new books and up-and-coming authors to these lists.

Readers have different comfort levels when it comes to the explicitness of sex and the level of sensuality in their books. Do not make any assumptions based on the age of the reader. Some readers like the sweet romances; some readers like the spicy ones. This is an important piece of information that we need to know when we're suggesting books to a patron. However, because sex is such a personal thing, we can't just blurt out, "How much sex do you like?" We need to be a little more subtle.

A fairly neutral way to ask this is to ask her if she likes sweet romances, or if she prefers spicy stories. Note the positive way of referring to both sweet and spicy romances. We are not saying one is better than the other. We are affirming that readers' tastes for both types of romances are valid. Most romance readers will understand the difference between sweet and spicy and will appreciate the fact that their librarian does too.

SUGGESTED WORDS TO DESCRIBE THE LEVEL OF SEX

Sweet	Spicy
Gentle	Hot
Innocent	Explicit
Mild	Steamy
Tame	Sensual

Make sure you ask the reader what authors she's enjoyed, and what she liked about that author's work. The reader may give you some clues about the level of sensuality she is looking for.

You must remember that many women feel embarrassed or apologetic about reading romances. Sometimes a reader wants a romance, but she doesn't want to come out and admit, especially to a librarian, that this is what she wants to read. She thinks we'll look down on her. Sometimes she is right. So she might use phrases such as "something light," or "beach book," or "something I don't have to think about," or "something about men and women." Sometimes she might even say she wants a love story, but not one of those silly romances. Sometimes she will actually admit that she reads romances but will do so with an apologetic, self-deprecating chuckle, as if she knows it's wrong, but it's something she can't help—like sneaking a handful of chocolate chips before they go into the cookie dough. I believe it is a pitiful state of things when a woman has to feel apologetic for enjoying stories about love and relationships.

When you meet a reader such as this, you might pick out some single title romances that have nonclench covers. Dorothy Garlock, Kristin Hannah, Megan Chance, Kathleen Eagle, and Penelope Williamson write romances that have a mainstream feel to them that may be reflected in the cover art.

If your reader is comfortable with a spicy book, you might want to suggest a Silhouette Desire or a Harlequin Temptation. In 1997, Harlequin Temptation launched a subseries of books called Blaze that are highly sensual and extremely explicit. There is no set schedule for these books, but they can be identified by the flames across the top of the front cover and the word Blaze on the spine. Blaze readers want highly sensual stories. In fact, I have heard readers complain that a particular Blaze book wasn't spicy enough.

If a reader wants a short, quick read, suggest an anthology or one of the shorter category romances: Harlequin Presents or Silhouette Desire if they are comfortable with a spicy read or a Harlequin Romance or Silhouette Romance if they prefer a sweeter story.

Sometimes patrons know what title they want, but don't want it if it's a romance.

LIBRARIAN:	May I help you?
WOMAN PATRON:	I'd like these three books please. *Shows Librarian a list of three books.*
LIBRARIAN:	Let's see. *Checks online catalog.* The new book by Michaelson is in, and so is the book by Terry Pratchett. And so is *The Bride Finder.* Let's go to the shelves and find them. *Librarian leads patron to the fantasy section and pulls a book off the shelf.* Here's the Michaelson book you wanted. Here's the Pratchett. *The Bride Finder* is in the romance section. That's over here.
WOMAN PATRON:	Romance? *Shudders dramatically.* I don't read romances. I thought these were all science fiction fantasy books. *Looks at her list in confusion.* They were recommended to me by a very well-read person.

The woman is obviously in a state of what the reference coordinator at my branch refers to as "romance denial." She wants the book, but not if it's a romance. This is a situation that many of us are probably familiar with. At this point, the librarian has some choices to make.

> She can shrug her shoulders and walk away.
>
> She can point out that although this branch has *The Bride Finder* cataloged as a romance, maybe one of the other branches does not and they can reserve a copy of a nonromance labeled book and have it sent over here for the patron.
>
> She can try to minimize the romance label effect by pointing out that this book is an award winner, even though it is in the romance section.
>
> She can offer to suggest other books the patron might enjoy.

To shrug one's shoulders and walk away, as tempting as it sometimes may be, is not a good solution. This does nothing to help the patron find the book she wanted to read. In offering to try to find a copy of the book that is not labeled as romance, the librarian takes on the role of an enabler, and does nothing to help allay the fears of the woman. To point out that the book is an award winner "in spite of being in the romance section," compounds the woman's impression that romances are lesser books. And while it is nice that the librarian is familiar with the RITA award winners, she must remember that the RITA is an award for the romance genre.

So much of RA work is dependent on the signals we get back from our patrons. If the woman gave me signals that she absolutely did not want to read a romance, I have to respect that decision. In that case, I might offer to suggest other books that she might enjoy.

But if she did not seem to dig in her heels, I might gently point out that *The Bride Finder* is an award-winning paranormal romance that many people have loved. I might also point out, gently and tactfully, of course, that if she loves fantasy but has never read a romance, then *The Bride Finder* would be a good choice because the fantasy element is just as strong as the element of romance. I would also mention that if she does read the book and enjoys it, to let me know and I'll be happy to suggest some other books that she might like.

We librarians have a professional responsibility to make the library a safe place for our romance reading patrons.

MAKING THE LIBRARY SAFE FOR ROMANCE READERS

Become romance-reader friendly.

Develop and maintain a romance collection, using professional standards.

House the romance collection appropriately.

Make sure all RA staff knows and understands the basics of the genre.

Include the romance genre in displays, promotions, and so on.

Wipe the term "bodice buster" out of your vocabulary.

Respect the reading choices of your patrons.

You'll probably find that after a while, patrons return to you again and again for suggestions. Librarians tend to build rapport with readers they've helped. A bond of trust is formed. We begin to learn exactly what our patrons like and what they don't like. When a new book comes in that we think a certain patron will enjoy, we make a note, mental or on paper, to mention it to them. I've found most readers are very appreciative of what they consider to be individual referral service. I think of it as giving me an excuse to push another book.

Sometimes we don't see romance readers because they are a fairly self-sufficient group of women. They are used to finding their romances on their own because it's easier than opening yourself to possible ridicule, especially if they're not very secure or self-confident about their own reading tastes. Some readers sit down with the new issue of *RT* and fill out reserve cards or place their own reserves. Sometimes we don't see romance readers because they've given up on us. We don't have the new releases. We don't catalog our romances, so they can't find what they need and we can't help them. So they go to used bookstores. But guess what? When we have our Friends of the Library book sales and sell paperback romances for a buck a bag, they buy them.

By our own attitudes about a genre—attitudes that are most likely based on false assumptions—we are responsible for alienating a large group of readers, most of them women. It is not unusual for a serious romance reader to read between five and ten books each week. And some librarians have alienated these women? What's wrong with this picture?

The Romance Reference Collection

In order to support romance readers' advisory, the three basic reference tools that should be in every reference collection are Gale's *What Do I Read Next? A Reader's Guide to Current Genre Fiction*, which comes out as a serial, and *Genreflecting: A Guide to Reading Interests in Genre Fiction* by Diana Tixier-Herald. A new edition of *Genreflecting* is expected in early 2000. Add Kristin Ramsdell's *Romance Fiction: A Guide to the Genre* (Libraries Unlimited 1999). These three books are essential in providing good readers' advisory, especially if the librarian is not confident of her genre knowledge.

Serious readers' advisors should also keep some variation of a romance readers' advisory notebook. Some libraries keep such information in an actual notebook, some libraries prefer to use a Rolodex, some use a box of file cards. The format is not important. What is important is that it is used, that it is a working tool. In order for it to be most useful, the information must be current, which means it must be frequently updated.

Fiction specialists should be aware of, if not subscribe to, some of the online discussion lists devoted to romance. Some lists are sponsored through fan Web sites, such as the list on All about Romance. Others began independently.

In the early 1990s, Leslie Haas, then a librarian at Kent State University and now the head of General Reference at Marriott Library at the University of Utah, felt there was a need for an online discussion group for romance readers. With the assistance of

---

**SUGGESTED LISTS TO INCLUDE IN YOUR
ROMANCE READERS' ADVISORY NOTEBOOK**

Current and past RITA finalists and winners

Affaire de Coeur Awards

Romantic Times Awards

Romance authors who live in your state and titles
of their books

Web addresses for romance sites

Read-alikes

Romances by topic

Popular continuing series in reading order

Kara Robinson, the cofounder of DorothyL, an online discussion group for mystery readers, she started Romance Readers Anonymous (RRA-L). In an e-mail, Haas told me, "My coworkers at the library [Kent State University] were skeptical, but with the success of DorothyL, thought it was viable. We took some ribbing, more about subject matter than the actual idea of a list. Both Kara and I thought we would be a success if we had twenty people sign up on the list. . . . Currently there are over 1500 subscribers." RRA-L is a heavy list where readers, writers, and librarians all gather to discuss the genre. To subscribe, send an e-mail to Listserv@Listserv.Kent.edu. In the body of the message, type "subscribe RRA-L" and you will receive information about the list.

More than Valentine's Day

Certain days and times of the year lend themselves to romance displays. While Valentine's Day and Sweetest Day are the most obvious, many other events can be reason enough to celebrate romance. Take advantage of these opportunities.

Displays don't have to be elaborate, and they don't have to stay up for weeks. Some displays can be set up in five minutes and left up until the end of the day.

Here's a hint. When you want to set out romances that take place during medieval times, for instance, go to the shelves and look at the covers. You will be able to immediately identify contemporary category romances by their distinct covers—their line look—so you can concentrate on the historicals. Most medievals have some sort of icon—a castle, a sword, a gauntlet—on the cover to let you know this is a medieval romance. Look at the clothing on the characters—medieval clothing and Regency clothing look nothing alike. Then skim the back cover copy. Trust me: this works, and it's very fast.

If you're doing a display of books about castles and knights, include a selection of medieval romances.

If you do displays that tie in to popular movies, don't neglect to include romances.

For the Rose Bowl, display a football surrounded by romances that have roses and other flowers on their covers.

When you create "local author" displays, bookmarks, or booklists, include romance writers.

Edgar Allen Poe's birthday is January 19. Set up a display of romantic suspense and thrillers. Cut some ravens out of black paper.

National Author Day is November 1. Put up a display of books of all genres by local authors. Include a bookmark listing all the authors from your state.

When you put up your St. Patrick's Day display, include romances that take place in Ireland.

In the middle of a blizzard, set out romances that have the ocean and sun and beach on their covers. Think warm. If you have a nice toasty quilt and a teacup and saucer for your display, so much the better.

Likewise, if you have a Christmas in July display, include Christmas romances.

Celebrate Jane Austen's birthday, December 16, with a display of her books and other Regency genre romances. Better yet, if you have a local author who writes Regency romances, invite her to be the guest speaker for a Regency tea.

Shakespeare's birthday is April 23. Display biographies of Will, Elizabeth I, Mary Queen of Scots, Walter Raleigh, and others. Include copies of the plays and sonnets, and don't forget video versions of his plays. Add some romances and other historical fiction set around that time period.

The RITA Awards are announced midsummer. Put up a display of the winning and finalist titles. If one of the finalists or one of the winning authors is from your area, make that a reason to celebrate. Be sure to write her a congratulatory note.

The first full week in May is National Pet Week. Put up a display of books about pets, and include romances that have dogs or cats on the covers.

Celebrate Bram Stoker's birthday, November 8, with a selection of vampire romances.

Annually, the Tuesday before Valentine's day is Dump Your Significant Jerk Day. Set out some romances and a box of chocolates.

Annie Oakley's birthday is August 13. Put up a sign that says "Wild Women of the West," and display Western romances.

The whole idea here is to be creative in thinking up reasons to celebrate romance. With a little bit of humor and a copy of *Chase's Calendar of Annual Events* (annual, Contemporary Books), most of us can come up with many more reasons to set out displays. But remember, always include romances.

6

What Romance Writers Think of Us

*M*any romance writers are library users. Many writers have children and bring them to the library to find information for their homework. Writers come to the library to find books on tape and videos and CDs. Because most writers are voracious readers, they come to borrow books. Just like regular people do.

Writers also use the library for research. Writers try to be scrupulous in their historical accuracy. If they make a mistake, they'll hear about it from their readers. Online writers' groups often have several threads about odd bits of historical details, from various styles of saddles, to different forms of address, to different styles of underwear—which can be very important to romance writers.

Writer Karen Harper often uses her library for her extensive research. She tells the story of a time she went into her local library in the small Florida community where she spends the winter. One of the librarians leaned over and whispered loudly to another librarian, "Here comes that interlibrary-loan lady."

Interlibrary loan is important to writers. Romance writers often need fairly obscure bits of information or books that are out of print. Several years ago, historical writer Deborah Simmons asked me to track down some books on the smuggling trade in eighteenth-century Cornwall. Cornish smuggling is not a hot topic at my branch. We didn't have anything on our shelves, and this was before the days of the Internet. Finally I found some titles, though OCLC only listed one or two copies in the United States. However, we were able to borrow them for her. She was thrilled. Now she could create a more accurate picture of that time and place in history.

We librarians are an important group of people to writers. Not only do we help them find information for their research, but we also introduce their books to readers. We suggest new authors, new titles. We encourage people to read. We have power.

Romance Writers of America usually has a booth at the conferences of ALA and also PLA, where librarians can find information about the genre. Often romance writers are present to autograph their books and talk with librarians who come up for a chat. At their annual conference, RWA announces a Librarian of the Year. In 1999, the librarian named was Alison Scott, head of the Popular Culture Library at Bowling Green State University in Bowling Green, Ohio. The Popular Culture Library houses the archives for RWA as well as many romance writers. It also collects genre romances.

In 1999, for the first time, RWA had a daylong preconference workshop for librarians and booksellers. Speakers included Jayne Ann Krentz; Alison Scott; Kristin Ramsdell, author of _Romance Fiction: A Guide to the Genre_ (Libraries Unlimited, 1999); and Joyce Saricks, coauthor of _Readers' Advisory Service in the Public Library,_ 2nd ed. (ALA, 1997). Approximately 150 librarians were present. RWA intends to make this an annual event before each national conference. This is an excellent professional growth opportunity for librarians who do readers' advisory.

Mary Jo Putney is a writer who loves librarians and dedicated her book _The Wild Child_ "To libraries and librarians: God bless you, everyone."

Susan Wiggs also loves librarians and dedicated her book _The Charm School_ to librarians:

To the most charming group of people I know:

Librarians,

You probably don't remember my name, but you saw me every week. I was the quiet child with the long pigtails and the insatiable appetite for Beverly Cleary, Carol Ryrie Brink, and Louise Fitzhugh. I was the one you had to tap on the shoulder at closing time, because I was still sitting on a stool in the stacks, poring over Ramona's latest adventures or sniffling as I read Anne Frank's diary. I was the little girl with the huge wire basket on the front of her bike—lugging home a stack of books that weighed more than she did. I never thought to thank you back then, because I didn't understand how very much all those hours, and all those good books, and all your patience meant to me or to the writer I would become. But I understand now. So this book is dedicated to you, to all of you, in gratitude for bringing books and readers together.

Several writers have featured librarians in leading or supporting roles that are always complimentary to the profession. Not a bun among them. See appendix F for a list of librarian characters in romances.

Looking for a Few Good Authors?

How can you find romance writers in your area? And what can you do with them once you've found them? If they have not already made themselves known to you, you'll have to track them down. This is not an onerous task.

Romance Writers of America is a national organization with local chapters throughout the United States. Though not all romance writers belong to RWA, most of us do. If you do not have Internet access, write or call the national office of RWA and ask for a contact person in your area. If you do have Internet access, simply log on to RWA's Web site and scroll down to the section for a listing of local chapters.

Invite romance writers to speak at Friends of the Library meetings or staff meetings.

If you have a local romance author, invite her to the library when new copies of her book arrive. Ask her to autograph them. Ask her to keep you informed about her new titles.

If there is a local romance writers' group in your area, offer to cosponsor a "How to Get Published" workshop for aspiring writers in your community.

If your library sponsors any kind of writing competition, invite local romance writers to judge.

Romance writers in Texas have a traveling author board (TAB). Writer Peggy Moreland says it's actually a display board on an easel. Posted on it are publicity photos, brief biographical material, and titles of books by local authors. The TAB is scheduled at different libraries in the area for a month at a time. It is picked up and delivered by members of the writers' group. Peggy says that the feedback from the libraries has been "tremendous and gratifying."

Romancing the Romance Author

When you've invited a writer to come to your library to do a program, include a book signing. There are several things you can do to make such a program a success. Most of these are common sense; however, after hearing many horror stories from writers, I have learned to make no assumptions.

Remember, your guest author is a professional and should be treated as such.

Make sure you publicize the event thoroughly, using newsletters, posters, bookmarks, media, word of mouth. Post flyers near your romance collection. Slip bookmarks for the event inside romances. If there's a romance-friendly used bookstore near you, ask the staff to hang up posters and hand out bookmarks announcing your event.

All staff should be familiar with at least some of your author's titles. Try to encourage them to read some of her books.

WHAT ROMANCE WRITERS THINK OF US

If your author is flying, meet her at the airport if necessary or pick her up at her hotel. If she is driving, make sure you have sent her a map or that she has directions to your library.

Expect your author and greet her when she arrives at your library. Show her where she can hang her coat and leave her purse—not in a public area, please. Show her where the rest rooms are located and offer her bottled water.

Do your homework. Have a prepared introduction. If there is to be a question-and-answer period following her presentation, have some intelligent questions ready to ask the author in case they're needed. If she hasn't already discussed it, ask her what she is currently working on or what her newest book is about.

For the signing, make sure you have copies of the author's books for sale and a staff member to take care of the cash register. Under no circumstances should you ask her to take care of the money, even if she is bringing books from her own supply to sell because her book is out of print.

Place the table where it is accessible. Ask the author if she prefers to sit at one side of the table or behind it.

Arrange her books attractively. Tablecloths are always nice; flowers are even better. When the signing is over, offer the flowers to the author.

Often authors bring their own book-signing pens, but just in case, offer a good pen—one that doesn't leak.

Have pens and slips of paper ready. When readers buy a book, they can write down the name of the person they want in the inscription. It is easier for the author to look at a name and write it than to hear a name and write it.

If you are overwhelmed by the number of people who want to buy books, first rejoice, and then practice polite crowd control.

When the program and book signing are over, thank the author graciously and see her to the door. Do not leave her to find her own way out of the building.

Follow up with a thank-you note.

Remember, even though romance writers are passionate about what they do, they are not happy little volunteers. They are professionals who are taking time away from their writing to do a program for you. Pay them an honorarium.

7

Ann's Five-Book Challenge

I believe in professional growth. I believe that all librarians should continually update their knowledge and skills. If we don't, we run the serious risk of turning into the little-old-lady kind of librarians that we all insist we are not. So in order to keep my hair out of a bun, every year I update my own knowledge of genre fiction. Every year I read at least five books in a new genre. For instance, in 1997 I read thrillers, in 1998 I read Westerns. In 1999 I am reading men's action novels. In 2000 I plan to read police procedurals, in 2001 fantasy, in 2002 science fiction. I will freely admit that I keep putting off reading horror books. I don't like to be scared.

Reading each different genre has given me an appreciation of that genre. I may not become a devotee—that's not the point—but I do become familiar with the genre. I gain a small understanding of what the books are about. I have also found some terrific writers I'd never have discovered otherwise. When a patron comes to the information desk and asks for the newest Elmer Kelton, I can say as I'm looking it up, "I haven't read this one yet, but I loved his *Cloudy in the West*." Then, as we're walking to the shelves, I can ask that patron what other Westerns they have found to be great reads. I add the answers to the Rolodex in my brain.

ANN'S FIVE-BOOK CHALLENGE

Five books is a small enough amount to be doable, yet enough to give me a taste of a genre. There are many places to find title suggestions. We have several books about different genres in our reference section. I often find myself going through them and making notes during lulls on the desk. Sometimes I ask genre readers to suggest authors I might try.

So I challenge you. Make the determination. Say it out loud: "This year I will read at least five romances."

Think of it as professional growth. Make sure you tell your supervisor so it can be noted in your evaluation.

And if you find a book that you think is simply terrific, let me know. I'm always looking for a few good books.

APPENDIX A

The RITA *Awards*

*N*amed for Rita Clay Estrada, one of the founding members of Romance Writers of America, the RITA Awards are presented annually by RWA to the best romance novels. Books with a publication date of the previous year are entered according to type and peer judged. A list of finalists is announced in the spring, both through press releases and on RWA's Web site. The finalists in each category are then peer judged again. The winners are announced at RWA's national convention in midsummer.

1999 Winners and Finalists

Best Traditional Series Romance
Sweet romantic novels. The word count for these novels is 40,000 to 60,000.

> *Monday Man* by Kristin Gabriel—*Winner*
> *The Boss, the Baby and the Bride* by Day Leclaire
> *And Cowboy Makes Three* by Martha Shields
> *Married by Mistake* by Renee Roszel
> *Stranded with a Tall Dark Stranger* by Laura Anthony
> *The Twenty-Four Hour Bride* by Day Leclaire
> *With This Child* by Sally Carleen

Best Short Contemporary Series Romance
Romantic novels in which sensuality may constitute a strong element. Word count for these novels is more than 70,000.

APPENDIX A

The Notorious Groom by Caroline Cross—*Winner*
Chase the Dream by Maris Soule
Courtship in Granite Ridge by Barbara McCauley
Just a Little Bit Pregnant by Eileen Wilks
Kids Is a 4-Letter Word by Stephanie Bond
The Lone Rider Takes a Bride by Leanne Banks
One Wicked Night by Jo Leigh
Tall Dark and Reckless by Lyn Ellis

Best Long Contemporary Series Romance

Romantic novels in which sensuality may constitute a strong element. The word count for these novels is more than 70,000.

Meant to Be Married by Ruth Wind—*Winner*
Baby on His Doorstep by Diana Whitney
Cowboy on the Run by Anne McAllister
Everyday, Average Jones by Suzanne Brockmann
The Family Next Door by Janice K. Johnson
For Christmas Forever by Ruth Wind
The Husband She Couldn't Remember by Maggie Shayne
The Rescue of Jenna West by Debra Cowan
The Wallflower by Jan Freed

Best Contemprary Single Title Romance

Romantic novels released as individual titles, not as part of a series. The word count for these novels is more than 70,000.

Dream a Little Dream by Susan Elizabeth Phillips—*Winner*
Call of Duty by Merline Lovelace
Garden of Dreams by Patricia Rice
Girl in the Mirror by Mary Alice Monroe
The Taming of Billy Jones by Christine Rimmer

Best Romantic Suspense/Gothic Romance

Romantic novels in which suspense is a major element of the plot. The word count for these novels is a minimum of 40,000.

Cool Shade by Theresa Weir—*Winner*

The Brother's Wife by Amanda Stevens

Holiday in Death by J. D. Robb

Homeport by Nora Roberts

If a Man Answers by Merline Lovelace

Ransom My Heart by Gayle Wilson

Return to Sender by Merline Lovelace

Best Paranormal Romance

Romantic novels in which the future, a fantasy world, or paranormal happenings are a major element of the plot. These may be single title releases or books published within established category romance lines fitting other category descriptions. The word count for these novels is a minimum of 40,000.

The Bride Finder by Susan Carroll—*Winner*

Aquamarine by Catherine Mulvany

Heaven's Time by Susan Plunkett

Legend by Laura Baker

This Time for Keeps by Kathleen Kane

A Well Favored Gentleman by Christina Dodd

Best Inspirational Romance

Romantic novels in which an inspirational message of personal religious faith is conveyed as a major element of the plot and not used as a plot device or a subplot. All inspirational books, both contemporary and historical, are eligible for this category. The word count for these novels is a minimum of 40,000.

Patterns of Love by Robin Lee Hatcher—*Winner*

Awakening Heart by Melody Carlson

The Best Christmas Ever by Cheryl Wolverton
Forgotten by Lorena McCourtney
The Fugitive Heart by Jane Orcutt
The Hidden Heart by Jane Orcutt
The Silver Sword by Angela Elwell Hunt

Best Regency Romance

Romantic historical novels with primary settings during the Regency period, typically 1800-1820. The word count for these novels is 40,000-85,000.

His Grace Endures by Emma Jensen—*Winner*
Best Laid Schemes by Emma Jensen
Celia's Grand Passion by Lynn Kerstan
Lord Heartless by Barbara Metzger

Best Short Historical Romance

Novels or sagas that have a strong romantic element throughout. The word count for these novels is 40,000-110,000.

Merely Married by Patricia Coughlin—*Winner*
Devil's Diamond by Constance Laux
Heaven Forbids by Karen Ranney
In His Arms by Robin Lee Hatcher
Nobody's Darling by Teresa Medeiros
Rachel LeMoyne by Eileen Charbonneau
Sleeping Beauty by Judith Ivory
The Tiger's Bride by Merline Lovelace

Best Long Historical Romance

Novels or sagas that have a strong romantic element throughout. The word count for these novels is more than 110,000.

My Dearest Enemy by Connie Brockway—*Winner*

Another Chance to Dream by Lynn Kurland
The Bad Luck Wedding Cake by Geralyn Dawson
The Bequest by Candice Proctor
A Kiss to Dream On by Stephanie Mittman
With Hope by Dorothy Garlock

Best First Book

A book entered in any of the other contest categories that is the author's first published novel is eligible for this award. If entered by a writing team, the book must be the first published novel for all members of the team.

My Darling Caroline by Adele Ashworth—*Winner*
A Father's Place by Joan Kilby
The Millionaire Meets His Match by Patricia Seeley
Oracle by Katherine Greyle
Priceless by Donna Schaff
Roses for Chloe by Elaine Grant
Stay . . . by Allison Leigh

1998 Winners and Finalists

Best Traditional Series Romance

His Brother's Child by Lucy Gordon—*Winner*
Her Secret Santa by Day Leclaire
Mommy and the Policeman Next Door by Marie Ferrarella
My Baby, Your Son by Anne Peters
Porcupine Ranch by Sally Carleen
Pregnant with His Child by Carla Cassidy
The Secret Baby by Day Leclaire
Wife without a Past by Elizabeth Harbison

Best Short Contemporary Series Romance

Nobody's Princess by Jennifer Greene—*Winner*

Bride Overboard by Heather MacAllister

Daddy by Accident by Paula Detmer Riggs

A Hard-Hearted Hero by Pamela Burford

Finn's Twins by Anne McAllister

Look What the Stork Brought by Dixie Browning

Mr. Valentine by Vicki Lewis Thompson

Twice the Spice by Patricia Ryan

Best Long Contemporary Series Romance

Reckless by Ruth Wind—*Winner*

The 14th and Forever by Merline Lovelace

Adam's Kiss by Mindy Neff

MacNamara's Woman by Alicia Scott

Nighthawk by Rachel Lee

Saving Susannah by Beverly Bird

The Twenty-Third Man by Peggy Nicholson

Best Contemporary Single Title Romance

Nobody's Baby but Mine by Susan Elizabeth Phillips—
Winner

Ask Mariah by Barbara Freethy

Finding the Dream by Nora Roberts

The Night Remembers by Kathleen Eagle

Best Short Historical Romance

Heart of a Knight by Barbara Samuel—*Winner*

All But the Queen of Hearts by Rae Muir

Indiscreet by Mary Balogh

Jake by Leigh Greenwood

A Knight to Remember by Christina Dodd

The Lady and the Knight by Lois Greiman
Once upon a Scandal by Barbara Dawson Smith
Outlaw in Paradise by Patricia Gaffney
Wonderful by Jill Barnett

Best Long Historical Romance

The Promise of Jenny Jones by Maggie Osborne—*Winner*
As You Desire by Connie Brockway
Brazen Angel by Elizabeth Boyle
The Guardian by Joan Wolf
My Sweet Folly by Laura Kinsale
One Perfect Rose by Mary Jo Putney
The Randolph Legacy by Eileen Charbonneau
Wild at Heart by Patricia Gaffney

Best Regency Romance

Love's Reward by Jean Ross Ewing—*Winner*
A Christmas Bride by Mary Balogh
The Temporary Wife by Mary Balogh

Best Romantic Suspense/Gothic Romance

On the Way to a Wedding by Ingrid Weaver—*Winner*
Better Watch Out by Dani Sinclair
For Your Eyes Only by Rebecca York
Framed by Karen Leabo
Night Whispers by Lynn Erickson
Secret Sins by Jasmine Cresswell
Until You by Sandra Marton

Best Paranormal Romance

Fire Hawk by Justine Dare—*Winner*
Dangerous Waters by Amy J. Fetzer

Heaven in West Texas by Susan Kay Law
Lost Yesterday by Jenny Lykins
Somewhere My Love by Karen Fox
Time Enough for Love by Suzanne Brockmann
Twice upon a Time by Emilie Richards

Best Inspirational Romance

Homeward by Melody Carlson—*Winner*
Brothers by Angela Elwell Hunt
Presumption of Guilt by Terri Blackstock

Best First Book

Brazen Angel by Elizabeth Boyle—*Winner*
Irresistible by Stephanie Bond
Lost Yesterday by Jenny Lykins
The Only Child by Carolyn McSparren
Remember the Time by Annette Reynolds
Winter Hearts by Maureen McKade

1997 Winners and Finalists

Best Traditional Series Romance

Her Very Own Husband by Lauryn Chandler—*Winner*
The Daddy Trap by Leigh Michaels
Ending in Marriage by Debbie Macomber
For the Love of Emma by Lucy Gordon
The Honeymoon Quest by Dana Lindsey
Temporary Husband by Day Leclaire
Undercover Daddy by Lindsay Longford

Best Short Contemporary Series Romance

Cowboy Pride by Anne McAllister—*Winner*
Angel on a Harley by Janis Reams Hudson
Charlie All Night by Jennifer Crusie
Christmas with Eve by Elda Minger
The Cinderella Deal by Jennifer Crusie
Family First by Marcia Evanick
Spring Bride by Sandra Marton

Best Long Contemporary Series Romance

Wild Blood by Naomi Horton—*Winner*
Expectant Father by Leanne Banks
The Fall of Shane MacKade by Nora Roberts
Having His Baby by Karen Young
His Runaway Son by Dee Holmes
Mackenzie's Pleasure by Linda Howard
Megan's Mate by Nora Roberts
My Fair Gentleman by Jan Freed

Best Contemporary Single Title Romance

Daniel's Gift by Barbara Freethy—*Winner*
Daring to Dream by Nora Roberts
Jackson Rule by Dinah McCall

Best Short Historical Romance

Always to Remember by Lorraine Heath—*Winner*
The Bartered Bride by Cheryl Reavis
Carried Away by Jill Barnett
Heart of the Hawk by Justine Dare
Sometimes Forever by Catherine Palmer

Sparhawk's Angel by Miranda Jarrett
The Wedding Raffle by Geralyn Dawson

Best Long Historical Romance

Conor's Way by Laura Lee Guhrke—*Winner*
The Bad Luck Wedding Dress by Geralyn Dawson
Denim and Lace by Patricia Rice
Gold Dust by Emily Carmichael
The Love Charm by Pamela Morsi
The Marshal and the Heiress by Patricia Potter
The Outsider by Penelope Williamson
Shattered Rainbows by Mary Jo Putney

Best Regency Romance

The Lady's Companion by Carla Sue Kelly—*Winner*
Miss Kendal Sets Her Cap by Marian Devon
Step in Time by Anne Barbour
The Unromantic Lady by Penelope Stratton

Best Romantic Suspense/Gothic Romance

See How They Run by Bethany Campbell—*Winner*
Last Night by Meryl Sawyer
Montana Sky by Nora Roberts
Reckless Lover by Carly Bishop
Woman without a Name by Emilie Richards

Best Paranormal Romance

Stardust of Yesterday by Lynn Kurland—*Winner*
Breath of Magic by Teresa Medeiros
Dream Catcher by Dinah McCall
The Faery Bride by Lisa Ann Verge

Frankly My Dear by Sandra Hill
A Ghost of a Chance by Casey Claybourne
Now and Forever by Kimberly Raye
The Wolf and the Woman's Touch by Ingrid Weaver

Best Inspirational Romance

The Scarlet Thread by Francine Rivers—*Winner*
Dreamers by Angela Elwell Hunt
Firestorm by Lisa Tawn Bergren

Best First Book

Stardust of Yesterday by Lynn Kurland—*Winner*
His Secret Side by Pamela Burford
Shadows on Velvet by Haywood Smith
Traveler by Elaine Fox

1998

In 1999 the membership of Romance Writers of America voted for their favorite book published in 1998. In alphabetical order by title, these are the top ten:

Baby I'm Yours by Susan Andersen
Dream a Little Dream by Susan Elizabeth Phillips
Kill and Tell by Linda Howard
The Last Hellion by Loretta Chase
Sealed with a Kiss by Pamela Morsi
Simply Irresistible by Rachel Gibson
Sleeping Beauty by Judith Ivory
Someone to Watch over Me by Ruth Owen
Tell Me Lies by Jennifer Crusie
Wedding Ransom by Geralyn Dawson

APPENDIX A

Several local chapters of RWA award excellence in romance novels. Books are entered and judged by booksellers and readers. The National Readers' Choice Award and the Holt Medallion are two such awards. The Science Fiction and Fantasy chapter of RWA annually awards the Prism Award to the best paranormal romance.

Romantic Times presents its Reviewers' Choice Awards at its fan convention. *Affaire de Coeur* also has an annual Reader-Writer Poll Award.

Some of the online electronic mailing lists have created their own awards based on their favorite books.

APPENDIX B

Read-Alikes

This list was first created by Susan Wiggs; then additions were made by Cathie Linz, Susan Elizabeth Phillips, and myself. (Librarians always quote their sources.) Feel free to turn these suggestions into bookmarks.

Jane Austen	Mary Balogh, Jean Ross Ewing, Karen Harbaugh, Candace Hern, Emma Jensen, Carla Kelly, Lynn Kerstan, Alicia Rasley
Maeve Binchy	Kristin Hannah, Joann Ross, Deborah Smith, Ruth Wind
Barbara Taylor Bradford	Megan McKinney, Erica Spindler, Katherine Stone
Sandra Brown	Stella Cameron, Suzanne Forster, Jennifer Greene, Linda Howard, Kathleen Korbel, Elizabeth Lowell, Karen Robards, Meryl Sawyer
Lois McMaster Bujold	Anne Avery, Susan Edwards, Dara Joy, Susan Krinard, Kathleen Morgan, Stobie Piel, Pam Rock
Tom Clancy	Suzanne Brockmann, Merline Lovelace, Lindsay McKenna, M. J. Rodgers
Mary Higgins Clark	Donna Ball, Beverly Bird, Bethany Campbell, Christiane Heggan, Laura Kenner
Robin Cook	Eileen Dreyer, Tess Gerritsen

APPENDIX B

Catherine Coulter	Connie Brockway, Stella Cameron, Patricia Gaffney, Judith Ivory, Susan Wiggs
Barbara Delinsky	Barbara Bretton, Katherine Kingsley, Cheryl Reavis, Teresa Weir
Jude Deveraux	Jill Barnett, Sandra Hill, Teresa Medeiros, Linda Lael Miller, Susan Sizemore, Deb Stover
Diana Gabaldon	Alice Borchardt, Megan Chance, Barbara Samuel, Ciji Ware, Susan Wiggs
Julie Garwood	Jill Barnett, Geralyn Dawson, Jillian Hunter, Sharon Ihle, Betina Krahn, Teresa Medeiros, Maggie Osborne, Rebecca Paisley, Patricia Roy
Olivia Goldsmith	Jennifer Crusie, Laura van Wormer
John Grisham	Jillian Carr, Jasmine Cresswell, Linda Markowiak
James Herriot	Leslie Brannen, Annie Kimberlin
Tony Hillerman	Catherine Anderson, Kathleen Eagle, Jean Hager
Tami Hoag	Margot Dalton, Lisa Gardner, Iris Johansen, Taylor Smith, Anne Stuart
Susan Isaacs	Janet Evanovich, Janice Kaiser, Carla Neggers
Jan Karon	Carla Kelly, Annie Kimberlin, Debbie Macomber, Pamela Morsi, Jodi O'Donnell

APPENDIX B

Jayne Ann Krentz	Janice Kaiser, Cathie Linz, Debbie Macomber, Susan Elizabeth Phillips
Joanna Lindsay	Christina Dodd, Lisa Kleypas, Elizabeth Lowell, Kat Martin
Terry McMillan	Angela Benson, Gwynne Forster, Shirley Hailstock, Sandra Kitt, Francis Ray
Larry McMurtry	Elizabeth Grayson, Leigh Greenwood, Robin Lee Hatcher, Lorraine Heath, Maggie Osborne, Patricia Potter, Ellen Recknor, Jodi Thomas, Penelope Williamson
Judith McNaught	Jill Barnett, Connie Brockway, Jaclyn Redding, Suzanne Robinson, Barbara Dawson Smith, Susan Wiggs
Barbara Michaels	Victoria Barrett, Margaret Chittenden, Kay Hooper
Belva Plain	Jennifer Blake, Rebecca Brandewyne, Roberta Gellis, Emilie Richards
Amanda Quick	Jo Beverley, Loretta Chase, Mary Jo Putney
Anne Rice	Michele Hauf, Linda Lael Miller, Maggie Shayne
Nora Roberts	Jennifer Greene, Rachel Lee, Susan Mallory, Susan Elizabeth Phillips, Emilie Richards, Ruth Wind
LaVyrle Spencer	Catherine Anderson, Deborah Bedford, Kristin Hannah, Lorraine Heath, Sandra Kitt, Jill Marie Landis, Stephanie Mittman, Cheryl St. John

APPENDIX C

Online Resources and Snail Mail Addresses

To say that the Web is continually growing and changing would be to state the obvious. Often we find a site address in a book and when we get there, it's gone. Nevertheless, these sites are worth knowing, are continually updated, and are credible.

www.rwanational.com

> Romance Writers of America homepage. This site has statistical information; a monthly listing of new releases; a database that can be searched by author, title, character names, character occupations, and so on. RWA also has a special area for librarians and booksellers. There are also links to author e-mail addresses and links to their homepages.

www.silcom.com/~manatee/utc.html

> Under the Covers reviews genre as well as nongenre books. Searchable by author, title, and subgenre.

www.thebooknook.com

> The Book Nook has articles and reviews. Is also part of a romance ring—a list of sites interconnected to each other.

www.mancon.com/genre/

> *Genreflecting* is a well-known print reference tool. The Web site is easy to use and covers various genres.

www.likesbooks.com

> Laurie Likes Books/All about Romance, a site full of articles, opinions, reviews, and lists.

www.bookbugontheweb.com

Bookbug has reviews, booklists, and links to many other romance sites.

www.anniekimberlin.com

I will post updates to the lists and other things in this book.

http://online.eku.edu/wcb/students/rfox/files/romancemain.htm

A "Web project dedicated to furthering undergraduate, graduate, and doctoral studies of mass-market romance novels published in the 1990's." The site includes such things as lists of academic papers on the genre, upcoming genre lectures, and calls for papers.

www.romantictimes.com

Romantic Times. Includes their awards, author profiles, reviews, articles, pseudonym search.

www.affairedecoeur.com

Affaire de Coeur.

www.co.henrico.va.us/library/romweb.htm

Love Letters: resources on the Web for fans of romantic fiction, which contains links to many more sites.

Romance Writers of America
3707 FM 1960 West
Suite 555
Houston, Texas 77068
(281) 440-6885 Phone
(281) 440-7510 Fax
info@rwanational.com

Affaire de Coeur
3976 Oak Hill Road
Oakland, California
94605-4931
(510) 569-5675 Phone
(510) 632-8868 Fax
sseven@msn.com

Rendezvous
1507 Burnham Ave.
Calumet City, Illinois
60409
(708) 862-9797

Romantic Times
55 Bergen Street
Brooklyn, New York
11201
(718) 237-1097 Phone
(718) 624-4231 Fax
rtmag@aol.com

APPENDIX D

Publisher Sites

*M*any publishers of romance have Web sites to share new releases and information about authors. Many of them invite readers—that includes librarians—to sign up for a newsletter and announcements of new releases.

Arabesque
www.msbet.com/property/arabesque

Ballantine
www.randomhouse.com/BB/loveletters/index/html

Barbour
www.barbourbooks.com

Kensington/Zebra books
www.kensingtonbooks.com

Leisure
www.dorchesterpub.com

Silhouette/Harlequin
www.romance.net

APPENDIX E

Rom-Speak: A Glossary of Genre Romance Terms

Alpha hero Hero who is a natural leader. Think Mel Gibson in *Braveheart*.

Americana Stories that take place in small-town America, usually somewhere in the Midwest. Secondary characters give the story much of its small town flavor. The stories are about ordinary people living ordinary lives.

Beta hero Think Jimmy Stewart in *It's a Wonderful Life*.

E-books Books that are published electronically. They are purchased by readers either on disk or by download. Readers read the books on their computer or on handheld readers that can hold several books. Though in its infancy, e-publishing—also called e-pubbing—has a loud voice.

Explicit Sexual encounters between the hero and heroine are described in great detail.

HEA ending Happily-Ever-After ending. One of the basic requirements for a genre romance.

Head-hopping A term used to describe an unsettled point of view. One minute the reader is in the heroine's head, next minute she's in the hero's head, next minute she's in the dog's head. Makes it difficult to know which character to identify with. Often drives readers nuts. Head-hopping seems to be common in general fiction.

Hot Describes a book that is highly sensual and very explicit.

Novella Novellas are approximately 25,000 words and are published in themed anthologies consisting of four or five novellas. Anthologies are great for giving a reader who wants something quick to read.

POV Point of view. A writing technique that allows the writer to show the character from the inside. Most romances are written with only two or three points of view: the hero, heroine, and perhaps a villain or other important secondary character. This allows the reader to strongly identify with the main characters.

RITA The annual awards presented by Romance Writers of America for excellence in romance writing. Named for Rita Clay Estrada, one of the founding members of RWA.

Rom Short for romance

Romance denial A state of mind in which either the patron denies reading romances even though she does, or the patron does not want to check out a book from the romance section. Romance denial usually comes from the erroneous belief that romances are "lesser" books, and this doesn't fit the patron's image of herself as a reader.

RT *Romantic Times*. A monthly fan magazine.

RWA Romance Writers of America, a professional organization for both published and unpublished romance writers. Currently the membership is over eight thousand.

Sensual Describes a book in which the author has used all the senses to create a strong atmosphere of passion. The sexual content may or may not be explicit.

Series book Often refers to a category romance. Not to be confused with a continuing series of books by a particular author or authors.

Single title A romance that can stand alone. It is not part of a series and may be either contemporary or historical.

TBR pile To-be-read pile. The stack of books you are planning to read. Romance readers have huge ones. Librarians should be able to relate.

Tortured hero A hero who has been emotionally wounded by traumatic events in the past. These wounds and emotional scars prevent him from accepting the love of the heroine until she is able to help him heal.

UBS Used book store.

APPENDIX F

Librarians as Characters in Romances

Abbie and the Cowboy by Cathie Linz. Silhouette 1996

An Angel for Emily by Jude Deveraux. Pocket 1998

Believing in Miracles by Linda Varner. Silhouette 1994

Bridal Blues by Cathie Linz. Silhouette 1994

Change of Heart by Cathie Linz. Silhouette 1988

Cinderella Twin by Barbara McMahon. Silhouette 1998

Cowboy for Christmas by Anne McAllister. Harlequin 1992

Emotional Ties by Laura Matthews. Avon 1984

And Father Makes Three by Laurie Campbell. Silhouette 1995

Flirting with Trouble by Cathie Linz. Silhouette 1992

Handyman by Cathie Linz. Silhouette 1991

Lightning That Lingers by Sharon and Tom Curtis. Loveswept 1991

Loving Lies by Ann Williams. Silhouette 1990

The Major and the Librarian by Nikki Benjamin. Silhouette 1999

Meant for Each Other by Cheryl Kushner. Precious Gems 1998

Midnight Jewels by Jayne Ann Krentz. Warner 1992

Miss Emmaline and the Archangel by Rachel Lee. Silhouette 1993

Moment to Moment by Barbara Delinsky. HarperPaperbacks 1998

Monday Man by Kristin Gabriel. Harlequin 1998

Morning Comes Softly by Debbie Macomber. Harper 1993

Out of a Dream by Marcia Evanick. Loveswept 1994

Perfect Partners by Jayne Ann Krentz. Pocket 1992

Pirate Princess by Suzanne Simms. Silhouette 1994

A Private Proposal by LaVerne St. George. Avalon 1990

Romeo and Julia by Annie Kimberlin. Leisure 1999

Rule Breaker by Barbara Boswell. Silhouette 1990

A Second Sunrise by Marjorie Eatock. Zebra 1995

Summer's Fortune by Joan Reeves. Meteor 1993

Surrender a Dream by Jill Barnett. Pocket 1991

Talk about Love by Deborah Shelley. Precious Gems 1999

Too Smart for Marriage by Cathie Linz. Harlequin 1998

The Truth Teller by Angela Elwell Hunt. Bethany House 1999

Truths and Roses by Inglath Caulder. Harlequin 1994

Wildfire by Cathie Linz. G. K. Hall 1996

The Woman in White by Jane Toombs. Silhouette 1995

Two novellas also feature librarians:

"The Crystal Heart" by Mary Kingsley in *A Valentine's Day Delight*, published by Zebra in 1994.

"Once upon a Dream" by Sally Laity in *I Do*, published by Barbour Press in 1998.

APPENDIX G

Book Lists

$\mathcal{I}$ love lists. As a reader, a list is a starting point, a place for ideas, a myriad of possibilities. As a librarian, lists are helpful—especially if I am not familiar with a genre—as an aid to doing collection development and readers' advisory, and to quickly making bookmarks. If I am very familiar with the area of the list, it's always fun to see how the listmaker's choice of titles differs from mine.

As of this writing, all these titles were in print. Look for updates and additions on my Web site: www.anniekimberlin.com

Humorous Romances

Because of You by Cathy Maxwell. Avon 1999

Best Laid Schemes by Emma Jensen. Fawcett 1998

The Bewitched Viking by Sandra Hill. Leisure 1999

Chasing Rainbow by Sue Civil-Brown. Avon 1999

Delight by Jillian Hunter. Pocket 1999

The Forbidden Lord by Sabrina Jeffries. Avon 1999

Hi Honey, I'm Home by Linda Windsor. Multnomah Pub 1999

Hint of Mischief by Katie Rose. Bantam 1998

Hooked by Stef Ann Holm. Sonnet 1999

I Thee Wed by Amanda Quick. Bantam 1999

The Kissing Stars by Geralyn Dawson. Sonnet 1999

Lady Be Good by Susan Elizabeth Phillips. Avon 1999

Soft Touch by Bettina Krahn. Bantam 1998

Truly Madly Yours by Rachel Gibson. Avon 1999

The Wedding Knot by Patricia Roy. Warner 1999

Contemporary Stories That Tug at Your Heart

Beauty and the Boss by Lucy Gordon. Harlequin 1999

Beyond Desire by Gwynne Forster. Arabesque 1998

Carried Away by Sue Civil-Brown. Avon 1997

Cattleman's Promise by Marilyn Pappano. Silhouette 1999

The Cowboy Is a Daddy by Mindy Neff. Harlequin 1999

Family Affairs by Sandra Kitt. Signet 1999

Halfway to Paradise by Neesa Hart. Avon 1999

Her Brother's Keeper by K. N. Casper. Harlequin 1999

The Long Way Home by Cheryl Reavis. Silhouette 1999

Mr. Right Next Door by Arlene James. Silhouette 1999

On Mystic Lake by Kristin Hannah. Crown 1999

Royal's Child by Sharon Sala. Silhouette 1999

A Rugged Ranchin' Dad by Kia Cochrane. Silhouette 1999

The Sexiest Man Alive by Sandra Marton. Harlequin 1999

Taming the Night by Paula Detmer Riggs. Ballantine 1999

What a Man's Got to Do by Lynnette Kent. Harlequin 1999

Historical Stories to Tug at Your Heart

The Color of the Wind by Elizabeth Grayson. Bantam 1999

Dauntry's Dilemma by Monique Ellis. Zebra 1999

Hannah's Heart by Jill Henry. Zebra 1999

A Kiss to Dream On by Stephanie Mittman. Dell 1999

Red Red Rose by Marjorie Farrell. Topaz 1999

A Stranger's Wife by Maggie Osborne. Warner 1999

Texas Splendor by Lorraine Heath. Topaz 1999

Paranormal Romances

Another Dawn by Deb Stover. Zebra 1999

Anywhere You Are by Constance O'Day-Flannery. Avon 1999

Believe by Victoria Alexander. Leisure 1998

Beyond the Highland Mist by Karen Marie Moning. Dell 1999

Bittersweet Summer by Rachel Wilson. Jove 1999

Body and Soul by Susan Krinard. Bantam 1998

The Bride Finder by Susan Carroll. Ballantine 1998

A Cry at Midnight by Victoria Chancellor. Leisure 1999

Eternal Sea by Alice Alfonsi. Jove 1998

Finding Mr. Right by Emily Carmichael. Bantam 1999

In the Midnight Hour by Kimberly Randell. Jove 1999

Lady Moonlight by Kate Freiman. Jove 1999

Nell by Jeanette Baker. Sonnet 1999

Snow in Summer by Tess Farraday. Jove 1999

Somewhere My Love by Karen Fox. Leisure 1997

Southern Charms by Trana Mae Simmons. Jove 1999

Virtual Heaven by Ann Lawrence. Leisure 1999

Wishes Come True by Kathleen Nance. Leisure 1998

Regency Romances

A Bird in Hand by Allison Lane. Signet 1999

The Best Intentions by Candice Hern. Signet 1999

The Captain's Courtship by Kate Huntington. Zebra 1999

The Hired Hero by Andrea Pickens. Signet 1999

His Grace Endures by Emma Jensen

Lucy in Disguise by Lynn Kerstan. Fawcett 1998

The Magnificent Marquess by Gail Eastwood. Signet 1998

Marigold's Marriages by Sandra Heath. Signet 1999

Miss Milton Speaks Her Mind by Carla Kelly. Signet 1998

The Poet and the Paragon by Rita Boucher. Penguin 1999

The Reckless Barrister by April Kihlstrom. Signet 1999

A Season of Virtues by Judith A. Lansdowne. Zebra 1999

The Unrepentant Rake by Melinda McRae. Signet 1999

Regency Period Historicals

The Bridegroom by Joan Johnston. Island Books 1999

The Gambler's Daughter by Ruth Owen. Bantam 1999

My Lord Stranger by Eve Byron. Avon 1999

One Night for Love by Mary Balogh. Dell 1999

The Runaway Princess by Christina Dodd. Avon 1999

Secrets of the Night by Jo Beverley. Topaz 1999

Someone to Watch over Me by Lisa Kleypas. Avon 1999

The Sound of Snow by Katherine Kingsley. Dell 1999

Too Wicked to Love by Barbara Dawson Smith. St. Martin's 1999

The Wild Child by Mary Jo Putney. Ballantine 1999

Romances with African-American Characters

Final Hour by Tracey Tillis. Onyx 1999

Forever Always by Jacquelin Thomas. BET 1999

Give and Take by Anna Larence. BET 1999

Hidden Memories by Robin Allen. Ballantine 1997

Made for Each Other by Niqui Stanhope. BET 1999

A New Day by Margaret Johnson-Hodge. St. Martin's 1999

Opposites Attract by Shirley Hailstock. BET 1999

Paradise by Courtni Wright. BET 1999

Sweet Honesty by Kayla Perrin. BET 1999

A Time to Love by Lynn Emery. BET 1999

Unconditional Love by Alicia Wiggins. Genesis 1999

Romances of the Later Nineteenth Century

The Charm School by Susan Wiggs. MIRA 1999

The Cowboys: Sean by Leigh Greenwood. Leisure 1999

The Diamond Rain by Constance Laux. Topaz 1999

If You Were Mine by Colleen Faulkner. Zebra 1999

Lark by Nora Hess. Leisure 1999

Maggie and the Maverick by Laurie Grant. Harlequin 1999

Simply Magic by Kathleen Kane. St. Martins 1999

Spirit's Song by Madeline Baker. Leisure 1999

With All My Heart by Jo Goodman. Zebra 1999

Medieval Romance

The Bartered Bride by Anne Avery. Bantam 1999

The Bride of Rosecliffe by Rexanne Becnel. St. Martin's 1998

Come the Morning by Shannon Drake. Kensington 1999

The Damsel by Claire Delacroix. Dell 1999

Dangerous Gifts by Haywood Smith. St. Martin's 1999

Dark Emerald by Lisa Jackson. Penguin 1999

Firebrand Bride by Janet Lynnford. Topaz 1999

The Irish Princess by Amy Fetzer. Kensington 1999

The Maiden's Heart by Julie Beard. Berkley 1999

Moonlight Mistress by Patricia Rice. Kensington 1999

Robber Bride by Deborah Simmons. Harlequin 1999

Silken Threads by Patricia Ryan. Topaz 1999

Taming the Lion by Suzanne Barclay. Harlequin 1999

Contemporary Stories

Contract Baby by Lynne Graham. Harlequin 1999

Eye of the Beholder by Jayne Ann Krentz. Pocket 1999

Heartthrob by Suzanne Brockmann. Fawcett 1999

Homeplace by JoAnn Ross. Pocket 1999

A Man for Mom by Sherry Lewis. Harlequin 1999

An Officer and a Hero by Elizabeth Ashtree. Harlequin 1999

Prince Charming's Child by Jennifer Greene. Silhouette 1999

The Right Man by Anne Stuart. Harlequin 1999

Stranger on the Mountain by Linda O. Johnston. Leisure
1999

The Sweetest Thing by Barbara Freethy. Avon 1999

Inspirational Romances

Charles Towne by Angela Elwell Hunt. Tyndale House 1998

The Dark Sun Rises by Denise Williamson. Bethany House
1998

Deep Harbor by Lisa Tawn Bergren. WaterBrook 1999

For Whom the Stars Shine by Linda Chaikin. Bethany House
1999

Hawaiian Sunrise by Lauraine Snelling. Bethany House 1999

Highland Call by Sharon Gillenwater. Alabaster 1999

Logan's Child by Lenora Worth. Steeple Hill 1998

The Perfect Groom by Ruth Scofield. Steeple Hill 1999

Roses for Regret by Audrey Stallsmith. WaterBrook 1999

Suddenly Married by Lorree Lough. Steeple Hill 1999

Adventure in All Times and Places

Brazen Heiress by Elizabeth Boyle. Dell 1999

Flowers under Ice by Jean Ross Ewing. Berkley 1999

Heart of the Jaguar by Lindsay McKenna. Silhouette 1999

Lady of Conquest by Teresa Medeiros. Bantam 1998

A Love beyond Forever by Diana Haviland. Leisure 1999

Moon over Water by Debbie Macomber. MIRA 1998

Pale Moon Rider by Marsha Canham. Dell 1999

A Pirate of Her Own by Kinley MacGregor. Harper 1999

The White Sun by Stobie Piel. Leisure 1999

Romantic Suspense

43 Light Street: Shattered Lullaby by Rebecca York. Harlequin
1999

APPENDIX G

Be My Baby by Susan Andersen. Avon 1999

Cause for Alarm by Erica Spindler. MIRA 1999

Conspiracy in Death by J. D. Robb. Berkley 1999

Dangerous Games by Justine Dare. Signet 1999

Every Breath She Takes by Suzanne Forster. Jove 1999

Half Moon Bay by Meryl Sawyer. Kensington 1999

Haunting Rachel by Kay Hooper. Bantam 1998

Interlude by Donna Hill. Genesis 1999

Jade Island by Elizabeth Lowell. Avon 1998

Keepsake by Antoinette Stockenberg. St. Martin's 1999

Lost to Love by Bridget Anderson. BET 1999

Love Lies and Alibis by Linda Markowiak. Harlequin 1999

Luke by Jennifer Blake. MIRA 1999

Murphy's Law by Marliyn Pappano. Silhouette 1999

Rage Factor by Chris Rogers. Bantam 1999

Redhawk's Heart by Aimee Thurlo. Harlequin 1999

Shadow Lover by Anne Stuart. Onyx 1997

Love in a Small Town

A Charmed Place by Antoinette Stockenberg. St. Martin's 1998

Head over Heels by Stephanie Mittman. Dell 1999

Hooked by Stef Ann Holm. Sonnet 1999

Romeo and Julia by Annie Kimberlin. Leisure 1999

Springwater Seasons; Jessica by Linda Lael Miller. Sonnet 1999

Sweeter than Sin by Kit Garland. Dell 1999

Sweetwood Bride by Pamela Morsi. Harpercollins 1999

Tell Me Lies by Jennifer Crusie. St. Martin's 1998

With Hope by Dorothy Garlock. Warner 1999

Yesterday and Forever by Vickie Presley. Jove 1999

APPENDIX H

Romance Authors with Multiple Pseudonyms

Laura Leone/Laura Resnick

Nora Roberts/J.D. Robb

Jayne Ann Krentz/Amanda Quick/Jayne Castle

Barbara Samuel/Ruth Wind

Margaret St. George/Maggie Osborne

Justine Davis/Justine Dare

Dinah McCall/Sharon Sala

Jennifer Greene/Jeanne Grant/Jessica Massey

Judith Arnold/Ariel Berk/Thea Frederick

Sharon and Tom Curtis/Laura London/Robin James

Ann Carberry/Sarah Hart/Maureen Childs/Kathleen Kane

Elizabeth Grayson/Elizabeth Kary

Kimberly Randell/Kimberly Raye

Shannon Drake/Heather Graham/Heather Graham
  Pozzessere

Madeline Baker/Amanda Ashley

Kathleen Korbel/Eileen Dreyer

Rachel Wilson/Emma Craig/Alice Duncan

Sue Civil-Brown/Rachel Lee

APPENDIX I

A Selection of Articles regarding the Romance Genre

BBB Research and Consulting, Inc. "Market Research Study." *Romance Writers' Report* (Dec. 1999): 15.

Beam, Alex. "The Soft-Focus Feminism of Romance Novels." *Boston Globe,* Nov. 5, 1997, sec. F, p. 1.

Carpenter, Betsy. "Living the Fantasy: Romance Writers Get Some Respect, Scholarly Interest and Tons of Readers." *U.S. News & World Report* (Nov. 6, 1995): 78.

Charles, John, Ann Bouricius, and Shelley Mosely. "Romancing the YA Reader." *VOYA* (Feb. 1999): 414.

Graham, Ellen. "Romances, Long Denied Reviews, Get Some Respect." *Wall Street Journal,* June 28, 1995, sec. B p. 1.

Hall, Libby. "Romstat 1998." *Romance Writers' Report* (June 1999): 20.

Herel, Suzanne. "Holy Harlequin! Christian Writers Recruited to Write Inspirational Romance Novels." *Mother Jones* (Jan./Feb. 1998): 17.

Kelman, Suzanne. "Heroine Addiction (Quest for the Perfect Romance Novel)." *Chatelaine* (Sept. 1995): 59.

Krentz, Jayne Ann. "All the Right Reasons: Romance Fiction in the Public Library." *Public Libraries* (May/June 1997): 162.

Linz, Cathie, Ann Bouricius, and Carole Byrnes. "Exploring the World of Romance Novels." *Public Libraries* (May/June 1995): 144.

McEnroe, Colin. "Unleash Your Inner Fabio: Reading Romance Novels to Understand Women's Thoughts." *Men's Health* (Sept. 1998): 90.

McLellan, Diana. "And Then He Ripped Off My . . ." *Washingtonian* (Feb. 1996): 58.

Mosley, Shelley, John Charles, and Julie Havir. "The Librarian as Effete Snob: Why Romance?" *Wilson Library Bulletin* (May 1995): 24.

Tunon, Johanna. "A Fine Romance: How to Select Romances for Your Collection." *Wilson Library Bulletin* (May 1995): 31.

Wexler, Diane Patrick. "The Many Sites of Love: Authors and Publishers Are Taking Advantage of the Many Amorous Opportunities in Cyberspace." *Publishers Weekly* (Nov. 11, 1996): 50.

APPENDIX J

A Selection of Books regarding the Romance Genre

Barron, Neil, Wayne Barton, Kristin Ramsdell, and Steven A. Stilwell. *What Do I Read Next 1997? A Reader's Guide to Current Genre Fiction.* 8th ed. Detroit: Gale, 1997.

Herald, Diana Tixier. *Genreflecting: A Guide to Reading Interests in Genre Fiction.* 4th ed. Englewood, Colo.: Libraries Unlimited, 1995.

Johnson, Victoria M. *All I Need to Know in Life I Learned from Romance Novels.* Los Angeles: General Pub Group, 1998.

Krentz, Jayne Ann, ed. *Dangerous Men and Adventurous Women: Romance Writers on the Appeal of the Romance.* Philadelphia: Univ. of Pennsylvania Pr., 1992.

Mussel, Kay, and Johanna Tunon, eds. *North American Romance Writers.* Lanham, Md.: Scarecrow, 1999.

Ramsdell, Kristin. *Romance Fiction: A Guide to the Genre.* Englewood, Colo.: Libraries Unlimited, 1999.

Saricks, Joyce G., and Nancy Brown. *Readers' Advisory Service in the Public Library.* 2nd ed. Chicago: ALA, 1997.

Index

INDEX

Ann Bouricius, a lifelong avid reader, is children's librarian with the Columbus (Ohio) Metropolitan Library System. There, she traces her path from snob to closeted romance convert to blazing zealot to published romance author. As Annie Kimberlin, she has authored three romance titles, *Lonely Hearts; Stray Hearts;* and her latest, *Romeo and Julia.* A passionate advocate for the romance genre, Bouricius presents workshops for librarians nationwide on romance fiction, and her articles have appeared in professional journals including *Public Libraries.*